BE MY DISCIPLES

VOLUME I

"…that we should be holy and without blame before him in love:"

Ephesians 1: 4

Jim Reynolds
1101 Witt Road
Cincinnati, OH 45255

AuthorHouse™
1663 Liberty Drive
Bloomington, IN 47403
www.authorhouse.com
Phone: 1-800-839-8640

First published by AuthorHouse   07/27/2010

ISBN: 978-1-4520-5364-6 (sc)
ISBN: 978-1-4520-5365-3 (e)

Library of Congress Control Number: 2010910446

Printed in the United States of America
Bloomington, Indiana

This book is printed on acid-free paper.

TABLE OF CONTENTS

INTRODUCTION

ADDENDUM

INTRODUCTION

The first three chapters of this book are strong and blunt. They were designed to be that way. If you can get past those three chapters without getting too upset you will begin to see the word of God in a most wonderful way. This seems like a strange way to write: knowing that most readers will be upset. However, I did not write this book in order to sell it. Therefore, I do not have to worry about running readers off. Seeing that no publisher would touch this book, I have undertaken this publication myself. Again, not to make a profit, but to place in the hands of those few to whom this book is intended.

Much of this book will challenge many previously conceived understandings learned through well meaning Sunday school teachers and pastors. As well meaning as these teachers and pastors are, they have in many ways distorted scripture to make the word of God more palatable to the congregations and for themselves. Thus, God has been presented as common and ordinary, rather than holy and sovereign as he truly is. Consequently, I have used many scripture references in an effort to let the scripture speak for itself; thus, refuting these distorted teachings on its own.

In addition, it is the church, and only the church that can present God to the world. If the church makes God less than whom he is; then the world will never come to know the true living God. A good church cannot present a Holy God to the world. Not even a great church can witness of a Holy God. Only a holy church can present a holy God to a lost and dying world. Anything less is sin. If it was a sin for Moses and Aaron not to present God as holy (sanctified) to the children of Israel; it is, likewise, a sin for today's church to present God as anything less than holy (sanctified):

> *And the Lord spoke to Moses and Aaron, Because ye believed me not,*
> *to sanctify me in the eyes of the children of Israel, therefore ye shall*
> *not bring this congregation into the land which I have given them.*
> *Numbers 20:12*

I have used some primitive stick figures to facilitate the reading. I purposefully made the stick figures as simple as possible so they don't compete with the material at hand.

Scripture quotes come from the King James Version of the Bible unless otherwise noted.

CHAPTER ONE

ON BEING WOMAN

God will get his will done even if we do the wrong thing, at the wrong time, at the wrong place. This is why God is God, because, getting his will done is not dependent upon our doing the right thing, at the right time, in the right place.

Please understand, God is much more concerned about our position than he is of our performance. In fact, if our position is correct then no matter how poor our performance, God will be honored (Luke 10:38-42). However, if we are out of position then no matter how good our performance, God is not honored (1Samuel 15:1-22). In fact, by being out of order, we in our zeal to perform may in reality be found to be in opposition to God himself. Consequently, position must be the paramount consideration for a Christian: not whether we do the right thing.

Marriage is a perfect illustration of how we are to be. Also, marriage is a perfect illustration of the order God wants for us to be in.

> *Wives, submit yourselves unto your own husbands, as unto the Lord.*
> *For the husband is the head of the wife, even as Christ is the head of*
> *the church: and he is the savior of the body. Therefore as the church*
> *is subject unto Christ, so let the wives be to their own husbands in*
> *every thing. Husbands, love your wives, even as Christ also loved*
> *the church, and gave himself for it; that he might sanctify and cleanse*
> *it with the washing of water by the word, that he might present it to himself*
> *a glorious church, not having spot, or wrinkle, or any such thing;*
> *but that it should be holy and without blemish. So ought men to love*
> *their wives as their own bodies. He that loveth his wife loveth himself.*
> *For no man ever yet hated his own flesh; but nourisheth and cherisheth*
> *it, even as the Lord the church: For we are members of his body, of his*
> *flesh, and of his bones, for this cause shall a man leave his father and*
> *mother, and shall be joined unto his wife, and they two shall be one flesh.*
> *This is a great mystery: but I speak concerning Christ and the church.*
> *Nevertheless let every one of you in particular so love his wife even as*
> *himself; and the wife see that she reverence her husband.*
> *Ephesians 5:22-33*

The husband walks out in a physical outward way Christ's relationship to the church. The wife in turn assumes the church's response to Christ. A good Christian marriage is a powerful outward physical manifestation of the entire Gospel of Jesus Christ. That is why Satan hates good marriages, because they are indeed a powerful weapon against him.

In this passage please note the order (or position) Paul uses. He clearly deals with the wife first then follows up with the husband; thus, making the order of the wife as paramount. If the wife is out of order, then the marriage is out of order. It doesn't matter how competent a wife is, or how incompetent a husband is, there is an order to the marriage, and it all starts with the wife.

Next, the husband represents Christ, and Christ did all the doings. He did it all. He was the doer likewise the husband is to be the doer. On the other hand, the church is the responder or the being person. Thus, the wife must be the being person. After all, what can the church do for God that hasn't already been done by Christ? He did it all. Sure he did, and because of that fact, the church is simply called to "be"; as in, "Be ye holy" (I Peter 1:16). Therefore, so must the wife "be" to her "doing" husband.

Come now ladies, bear with me here. Actually, the wife is the favored of the two in a marriage. Continue with me, and I will show you.

Remember, position (order) is the issue (just re-read that passage, Eph. 5:22-33, and pause at each position statement). Sorry, but that is the way God made it, wrote it, said it, and God will not change it. Not even for the wives who can "do" better than their husbands. Wives get in position and God will straighten out the husband.

Because you represent the church and the church is the responder to her head, which is your husband. The husband represents Christ, who is the head. Thus, your husband is automatically your head. God made him your head. So, whether your husband is doing a good job or not doesn't make him any less your head. Your husband is your head, period. That has already been decided. Now, you have to make a decision (or a response): Will you submit or not?

Sorry, your husband is already in order. He is your head. That happened the very moment you became husband and wife. He may not be a good head, but he is your head nevertheless. He is already in proper position. Let me explain: In the garden of Eden God first formed the man. In so doing God "breathed into his nostrils the breath of life" (Gen. 2:7). On the other hand, when God made Eve he operated differently, and this distinction is significant.

However, in no way does this make a woman inferior in value to a man. Man and woman are equal in the sight of God. The two simply have different order and function, but I repeat both are just as valuable.

When God formed woman; "He took one of his ribs...and the rib, which the Lord God had taken from man, made he a woman" (Gen. 2:21-22).

Notice, Adam received his essence directly from God, whereas, Eve received her essence from Adam. Adam had a direct connection to God, whereas Eve becomes dependent upon Adam for her spiritual substance. I realize that women will cringe at such a notion. However, is this not a perfect picture of the church's relationship to God? We, like Eve, must go by way of Jesus, our head, to reach God the Father.

In Genesis 2:23 Adam said, "This is now bone of my bones, and flesh of my flesh... therefore, shall a man leave his father and his mother, and shall cleave unto his wife; and they shall be one flesh." In Ephesians, Paul writes almost the exact same thing after discussing the marriage relationship and the church's relationship to Christ: "For we are members of his body, of his flesh, and of his bones. For this cause shall a man leave his father and mother, and shall be joined unto his wife, and they two shall be one flesh" (Ephesians 5:30-31).

Then Paul adds: "This is a great mystery: but I speak concerning Christ and the church" (Eph. 5:32).

There can be no mistake. There is a connection here: a very important connection. It connects Genesis to all the rest of the Bible. Let us take another look at these verses: Genesis 2:21-24 and Ephesians 5:30-32.

Adam said...therefore shall a man leave his father and his mother, and shall cleave unto his wife: and they shall be one flesh.

For this cause shall a man leave his father and mother, and shall be joined unto his wife, and they two shall be one flesh. This is a mystery: but I speak concerning Christ and the church.

Now, break this down even further:

Adam said....

...this is a great mystery...Christ and the church.

Then let us put these together: "Adam said: but I speak concerning Christ and the church." From the Garden of Eden the first Adam could see the last Adam on the cross of Calvary. Let me explain by quoting the Apostle John as he witnessed the crucifixion that day on Calvary.

...when they came to Jesus, and saw that he was dead already, they break not his legs: But one of the soldiers with a spear pierced his side, and forthwith came there out blood and water. And he that saw it bare record, and his record is true: and he knoweth he saith true, that ye might believe.

John 19:33-35

3

It was at that moment John saw "the mystery" that Paul would later write about in Ephesians. That is why John exclaimed in such a profound way: "and he that saw it bare record, and his record is true: and he knoweth that he saith true, that ye might believe:" (John 19:35)

The blood and water that came forth from the wound in Jesus' side was the church. Thus, the bride of Christ was born that day on the cross. The bride of the first Adam also came the same way: "And the Lord God caused a deep sleep to fall upon Adam, and he slept: and he took one of his ribs, … And the rib, which the Lord God had taken from man, made he a woman, and brought her unto the man" (Gen.2:21-22). Just as Eve was taken from within the first Adam's side, the bride of Christ likewise came from within the last Adam's side. That hour on the cross on Calvary, the Lord breathed his last. Thus, a deep sleep came over him (a three day sleep, but a sleep just the same). Just as God took Eve from the side of Adam, the bride of Christ, the church, was taken from the side of the last Adam. To this day both Adams have the same scar in their sides. Therefore, we, the bride of Christ, are as close to our Lord as Eve was to Adam. From within Adam came Eve; then Adam was found in Eve. So too are we in Christ, and he in us.

Look closer. What is the "this" in "this is the great mystery" (Eph.5:32)?

Sure, it is the same thing that John the Apostle saw there at the cross of Calvary; and why John was so excited and swore three times, and was so sure that those that could see it would believe too. That day in the Garden of Eden Adam could look ahead and see Calvary. Likewise, the Apostle John along with Paul could look back to Adam and Eve in the Garden. The two events were one. Now, couple this with: "the two shall be one flesh". Thus, the church is as close to the living God as Eve was to Adam!

Paul puts it another way:

And so it is written, the first man Adam was made a living soul; the last Adam was made a quickening spirit. How be it that was not first which is spiritual, but that which is natural; and afterward that which is spiritual. The first man is of the earth, earthy: the second man is the Lord from heaven. As is the earthy, such are they also that are earthy: and as is the heavenly, such are they also that are heavenly.

And as we have born the image of the earthy, we shall also bear the image of the heavenly.

I Corinthians 15:45-49

Now, do you understand?

UNITY! Sure, unity is the "this" that Paul is talking about, perfect unity with God!

Yes, Paul says, "I speak concerning Christ and the church" (Eph.5:32). However, the overriding aspect is the nature of this relationship or position that the church has to God and that is one spirit in the same manner as Adam and Eve were one flesh.

This is the same oneness that Jesus spoke of to his disciples the night before Calvary:

At that day ye shall know that I am in my Father, and ye in me, and I in you.

John 14:20

Also, in our Lord's Prayer to the Father that same evening he said:

And the glory which thou gavest me I have given them; that they may be one, even as we are one: I in them, and thou in me, that they may be made perfect in one…

John 17:22, 23

How glorious, our relationship to our Lord is perfect unity; perfect oneness: just as Adam had with Eve.

And they were both naked, the man and his wife, and were not ashamed.

Genesis 2:25

What a beautiful verse. That verse is the perfect description of happiness. And this is how a Christian marriage should be even today, "not ashamed". However, look around. What do you see?

I'm not asking you to look at the world. Simply look within the church, and I am not saying to look with a critical judgmental eye: Just look, and if you're honest with yourself, you will want to cry.

What is wrong?

Look at the very next verse: **"Now the serpent…"** (Gen.3:1).

Thus, the crux of the matter:

5

What was the devil after? Sure, he was after that unity. Today he is after this same unity. After all, what does Paul say immediately after dealing with the order of the marriage, order of the family, and the order in the work place? "...stand against the wiles of the devil" (Eph.6:11), because where you find unity, you'll find the devil.

No question about it, unity stands in direct opposition to Satan himself. Without unity the church cannot stand, nor can a marriage. For only through unity shall Satan be defeated: unity of woman to man, and unity of the church to Christ.

Now, how did the devil go about destroying the unity of Genesis 2:25? He went after the woman, not the man: "...and he said unto the woman" (Gen.3:1). And he didn't waste anytime about it either.

How did he deceive the woman? The same way he is doing it today, "...ye shall know good and evil" (Gen.3:5); or in today's vernacular, "...ye shall know right from wrong". To disrupt the unity, the devil talked the being person into doing. Please note: He was able to get Eve to do a good thing. After all, "...the tree was good for food" (Gen.3:6).

It is this very fact that makes Satan's scheme so very successful. The woman is very capable, and usually does a good job at whatever she undertakes. In fact, she even does an excellent job. Women for the most part are more capable than men. They are quicker thinkers, and have greater insight, and overall their minds are sharper (Sorry guys, this is the way it is).

God made woman this way because, she was to be the creative genius, and not solely in bearing children. The woman is to be creative in all she does. However, she can only be who she is meant to be while she is in proper position; which is in submission to the man.

God did not set it up this way to punish the woman. No, she is to be in submission, because she will need all of her faculties to be her creative self. Consequently, God made her the weaker sex (I Peter3:7), so she could better assume her proper place. She is weaker not only physically, but spiritually as well.

Yes, you heard me correctly.

Adam received his spirituality directly from God. Eve received hers' from Adam:

> *For a man indeed ought not cover his head, forasmuch as he is the image and glory of God: but the woman is the glory of the man. For the man is not of woman; but the woman of the man. Neither was the man created for the woman; but the woman for the man.*
>
> *I Corinthians 11:7-9*

Therefore, the place for her to be creative is in submission to her husband.

I can't, I just can't.

But I suffer not a woman to teach, nor to usurp authority over the man, but to be in silence... Adam was not deceived, but the woman being deceived was in the transgression.

I Timothy 2:12-14

Satan knows what he is doing. He went after the woman because she is the easiest to defeat (That is if she is out of order). The reason for this is with her quick mind, she is so easily tempted, especially by goodness and rightness.

That is exactly how Satan deceived Eve that day in the garden. Today it is the same in our churches. Women see a problem, and see the solution, and instantly they put the two together. However, the woman is way ahead of the husband; and out of order as well. In solving the immediate problem she so often creates a bigger problem in the end.

Ladies, God doesn't need your goodness and rightness. Your husband is to do all the doings. He is to handle the check book, as well as the income taxes. He should be the one to deal with the bill collectors. As well as, getting the car fixed, and wait for him to answer the doorbell.

By having the man do all the doings, you are now free to be who God intended you to be. That is what scares Satan: the prayers of a submissive woman. That is why Satan continually tempts you gals to "do": So you won't "be".

Once in order, you will see the wisdom of God letting you be a woman. Then you will experience "this mystery" of unity with God. The one flesh of Genesis 2:25 will come alive to you (spiritually). You will then be in perfect union with the last Adam. Thus, "At that day ye shall know that I am in my Father, and ye in me, and I in you" (John 14:20).Then, along with the Apostle John, you too will be able to say, "I bare record, and this record is true, and I knoweth that I saith true, that ye might believe" (John 19:35)...that we are indeed one with him.

CHAPTER TWO

ON BEING MEN

Now is the time to deal with the men. I am going to switch gears here, so don't get too flustered. After all, men are the doers, and this section is the doing section; therefore, we will deal with doing, and by concentrating on doing rather than being, things will go at a much faster pace. So, get ready.

First, please take another look at Ephesians 5:22-23. This time let us look at the man's responsibilities. We will see that the husband's duties are all action packed:

> *Husbands, (love) your wives, even as Christ also (loved) the church, and (gave) himself for it; that he might (sanctify) and (cleanse) it with the (washing) of water by the word, that he might (present) it to himself a glorious church, not having spot, or wrinkle, or any such thing; but that it should be holy and without blemish. So ought men to (love) their wives as their own bodies... For this cause shall a man (leave) his father and mother, and shall be (joined) unto his wife.*
>
> *Ephesians 5:25-28, 31*

Men, since you are the doer, let's get started doing. After all, the gals are now busy being who God intended them to be, you men are now free to "do".

You now have full custody of the checkbook. Right? ... You do handle all the finances, don't you? Well, don't you?

Well, ugh...Sure, I mean, after all, we are the men of the house, aren't we?

Good! In fact, you are now free to handle all the actual transactions between the family and the outside world. Sure, it is a hassle dealing with all the ends and outs of running a marriage and family, but why do you suppose God gave you those big shoulders. That's right you are to deal with each and every hassle that comes your way. And you know what? The outside world won't know how to deal with you men, because they are so geared towards dealing with women. The outside world gets all flustered when a man keeps answering the door. They especially get disjointed when the man keeps answering the phone. Try it and you will see what I mean.

At first the wives miss answering the phone, but ladies, relax and enjoy your husband doing his thing. In fact gals, you will down right enjoy having a man around doing something other than taking out the garbage, and mowing the lawn.

Hey Buddy, is that all you think I'm good for...to be a Butler...Ugh?

Be honest with me. Do you really handle the finances? Do you sincerely deal with all the worldly intrusions into your marriage and family?

If you are totally honest; most of you still haven't completely assumed the most minor of tasks that you were designed by God to "do" (And, I am not talking about fixing the car or unstopping the sink). How can you expect to do more than butler tasks if you aren't doing the basic tasks at hand? Sure, God has bigger and better things for you to do, but first you must be faithful in the little before God can entrust you with greater things. In addition, I'm sure there are still struggles between you and your wife over even the simplest of tasks, such as the checkbook.

You get that checkbook in your control, and then watch God move you on to bigger and better things.

OK husbands, let's talk turkey. What is the real problem here? I mean, lets quit playing mind games with one another. Let's get down to the nitty-gritty. Your real problem isn't your wife. It isn't that you feel like a butler, or just a handyman around the house. Your problem is the TV.

TV?

What does the TV have to do with my being a Godly man?

Everything! However, I am not going to go into all the evils of television. You already know why TV is bad for you. You already know that TV is to the church what cigarettes are to cancer. You have already seen all the statistics about the corruption of TV upon our lives. There are studies and studies about how TV is destroying us, yet in almost every Christian home you go into there it is, the center of attraction. It occupies the most prominent position in the house.

Oh, we don't watch it that much...only the good programs.

If that be the case: "What meaneth then this bleating of the sheep in mine ears, and the lowing of the oxen which I hear." (I Samuel 15:14)

King Saul defended himself just as you have: "And Saul said, they have brought them from the Amalekites: For the people spared the best of the sheep and the oxen, to sacrifice unto the Lord thy God; and the rest we have utterly destroyed." (I Samuel 15:15)

Just like Saul, you only watch the best TV has to offer. You don't watch those "bad" programs. In fact, you campaign against the filthy shows that come on TV. You might even write letters of protest to the sponsors, and on some occasions you have even boycotted the products of those sponsors that don't listen to your verbal complaints. No Sir, you don't watch those bad shows; no way.

Then tell me, why are the viewing habits of the church no different from the viewing habits of the rest of the country? That's right there is no difference (<u>Who Speaks For God?</u>, by Chuck Colson, Crossway Book, Westchester, Illinois, 1985, p.130).

Pray tell Christian; why even keep the best of what TV has to offer? All the programs come from the same source. Just as God did not want the best the Amalekites had; God does not want the best Hollywood has to offer. Come now, consider the source.

I want you to please take note as to who it was that finally killed Saul. It was an Amalekite. Also notice that the same Amalekite took King Saul's crown and bracelet (II Samuel 1:6-10). All because King Saul kept the best of what the world had to offer. The same thing is happening to you right now. Yes, the best of TV is slowly stealing your crown from you, and you don't even know it.

When is the church going to wake up to the fact that we cannot compromise with the world, flesh, and the devil? We are not to even tolerate the best that they have to offer. We must do as Samuel did:

> *Then said Samuel, bring ye hither to me Agag the King of the Amalekites. And Agag came unto him delicately. And Agag said, surely the bitterness of death is past. And Samuel said, as thy sword hath made women childless, so shall thy mother be childless among women. And Samuel hewed Agag in pieces before the Lord in Gilgal.*
> *I Samuel 15:32-33*

So too must we do to that idol that sits in the most chosen place of our Christian homes.

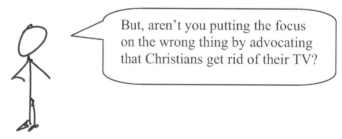

But, aren't you putting the focus on the wrong thing by advocating that Christians get rid of their TV?

Not at all: You see, TV is addictive, and falls into the same category as alcohol. Just as you can't deal with an alcoholic until they are dried out, you can't deal with Christians concerning spiritual matters until their minds have been deprogrammed from that TV.

For too long, I have hedged about bringing up this touchy subject matter with Christians. However, that is no longer the case, because time is too short now. Men, you must do as Samuel did. You must get rid of that Amalekite or it will be your downfall. It will, believe me, it will; and you know it men. In fact, you have thought about getting rid of that thing many times. I know you have, but you worry about what people will think. More than that, however, your wife will be your major hurdle. I know for I have seen it happen.

A seminary classmate of mine had had enough of that boob-tube. So, he picked up his TV, went downstairs and put it in the dumpster. His wife became so upset that she went and found her husband's two best friends. After hearing this horrible story from this distraught wife, they rushed over to talk some sense into their friend. After all, what are friends for? (I am not exaggerating for it happened just as I am describing it here).

These two friends argued and rationalized with this young man for thirty minutes. The whole time the wife was overseeing from the second floor balcony. Finally, the dejected beaten husband picked the TV out of the dumpster (That was the dead give away: He had placed the TV in the dumpster rather than throwing it in). He then took the idol back and placed it on that choicest spot in the apartment to be worshipped ever more. Reluctantly worshipped, but worshipped nevertheless.

Sure, you could go on and on rationalizing and arguing for the TV, just like those two friends at seminary, but I am not going to address these issues, because these questions have been addressed over and over again. Yet, no one gets rid of their TV. Face it, TV is an idol. Men, the real issue is: Are you going to be like Adam and let Eve deal with the devil, or are you going to be the husband you are meant to be, and do what you know needs to be done?

I have been without a TV for over thirty years now, and I can honestly and sincerely say that it was the single most important decision I made in my spiritual life. Up until then, I was simply treading water spiritually.

I can't emphasize this issue enough. I can give you study after study of the affects of TV on your mind and life, but only the revelation of the Holy Ghost will truly work. However, for most of you men, you already know that TV is suffocating your spiritual life. You don't need anymore reasons or proofs. You simply need to do what you already know to do.

For years, I had known that TV was hindering my relationship with God, but I couldn't turn it off. Then I read David Wilkerson's first book, The Cross and Switchblade, and it was there that he too said that his spiritual life didn't manifest itself until he threw out his TV. Shortly thereafter, his ministry was off and running.

That was all that I needed. The next day I announced to my family that I would be getting rid of the TV in one month. I didn't mention this subject again until two weeks later. Just as the first time, I told my wife and the two boys at the dinner table, "In two weeks I would be getting rid of the TV." I wanted them to know that this wasn't a spur of the moment decision. This decision wasn't based on feelings, but was a deliberate rational decision, and I wanted them to be prepared. Hopefully, they would be more understanding.

A week later, I made the announcement again, "One week from now there will be no more TV." Then, each day of that week I gave the count down:

"Six more days and the TV will be gone."

"Five more days..."

Until finally: "Tomorrow the TV will disappear."

Then came the eventful day, and don't you know, they had not believed me! They honestly were taken by surprise. In fact, all three of them were shocked when they came home that evening and found no TV. It was as if I had never warned them. Unbelievable!

Worse yet, I heard about it for months afterwards. Not so much from the boys, but from my wife. For two solid months she reminded me about not being able to relax in front of the TV. I would not be moved.

However, in defense of my wife, she did come around, and today she stands solidly with me on this issue. Yes, all our relationships improved once that idol was destroyed.

Please know, men, it is your job to do this; not the wives. Men, if it is to be done, you will have to do it. Also realize, you will get all sorts of criticism, but you too will see that it is worth it.

Again, I say, be honest with yourselves. You know what is what. You don't need anymore facts on the matter. Just do it. OK men, we are finished.

Yep, you become the busy doer around your house, and the Lord will lead you from there. I'm not saying that once you get the checkbook in hand and throw out the TV that your job is done. I'm saying, now your job has just begun. I'm also not so naïve to think that anyone will actually do what I've suggested here. In all the years that I've advocated getting rid of the TV; only a handful have done so. Now I understand why the Old Testament prophets and kings had such a difficult time in getting the people to destroy their idols. "Jim, it's only an inanimate object." No, my friend, TV is an idol. Think about it.

What is the problem, ladies?

As if you don't know.

Here you go into such detail with the gals…But you're so easy on the guys. That's not fair.

OK, let's talk. You want to know what the real problem is.

Well yes, what is the real problem?

The real problem is that most Christians don't want to go to heaven…at least, no time soon. I'm talking both men and women. The truth is most folks (church goers) want to get their heavenly credit card (salvation) then live happily ever after here on this earth. Oh, these are good people we are talking about. They don't lie, steal or do any of those bad things. In fact, these are the good active church goers. They read their Bible, pray often, and attend church faithfully. You might say they are very religious. In fact, outside church these same folks are hard working citizens of the community. We are talking good people here, good solid "Christians". However, one thing is missing, and that is URGENCY, a sense of urgency. These good people simply lack a sense of urgency in their lives.

As good as these people are they aren't in a hurry to get to heaven. All things considered, they like it right here where they are. They are comfortable and intend to keep it that way. Besides, if anything should go wrong in the here and now, they have their heavenly credit card handy.

If there is urgency the urgency is for God to solve a problem for them. The urgency has nothing to do with wanting to be with the Father in his kingdom. They want the peace of God, but they aren't interested in the God of that peace.

Zechariah, chapter seven, speaks to this.

CHAPTER THREE

ON BEING THE CHURCH

They refused to hearken, and pulled away the shoulder, and stopped
their ears, that they should not hear. Yea, they made their hearts as
an adamant stone, lest they should hear the law, and the words which
the Lord of hosts hath sent in his spirit by the former prophets:
Zechariah 7: 11-12

Zechariah was part of the rebuilding crew in Jerusalem after the seventy year captivity in Babylon. The rebuilding of the temple had been a slow unsure proposition, and some doubted that the temple would ever be rebuilt, or that God even wanted it done. Had God forsaken them?

So devastating was the destruction by the Babylonians that the children of Israel weren't sure about anything anymore. However, the work persisted from Ezra and Nehemiah to Haggai until the people could finally see some definite progress, and a ray of hope shinned through the rubble. The workers were actually beginning to think: Could it be that God hadn't forgotten his people after all?

The rebuilding work picked up pace. In fact, the word of God to the prophet Zechariah was indeed a message that God was truly their God. Each message God had Zechariah preach was more encouraging than the last. Finally, Zechariah preached of the coming Messiah. Nothing could have been more reassuring to this rag-tag bunch of the faithful. God had remembered them. They were still his chosen people.

So profound and uplifting were Zechariah's words that news filtered back to those many Jews that remained in Babylon. And it wasn't long before there arrived a contingent of Jews form Babylon to see for themselves.

The sophisticated contingent came to Jerusalem with a hidden agenda. However, it didn't take Zechariah long to sniff out their true motive. Not for one minute had this contingent from Babylon fooled Zechariah, and he was quick to tell them so.

Everybody loves a winner, and now that the temple was rebuilt, and would again be a showplace for the world to see: Now that the prophets of God were preaching positive uplifting messages: Now that things were getting better the ones that stayed behind wanted to get in on all the glory. However, it appears the contingent wasn't aware of their own hidden motives.

This same lack of understanding is also so typical of the New Testament church. So many well meaning church members, doing well meaning tasks, have no idea what they are doing is actually standing in direct opposition to God.

As a prophet, how do you tell them? How do you tell well meaning church members that their prayers are to no avail? How do you tell these that their fasting is self seeking? The prophet doesn't want to be harsh or offensive. On the other hand, the prophet cannot overlook this abject sin. Yes, abject sin: Because it is so hard to recognize makes the sin of propriety (goodness) the very worst kind of sin. It is easy to see the sin of the drunk in the street. It is another thing to see the sin of those in the pews. Once seen, it is nearly impossible to tell the well meaning church member that they are in fact sinning. Therefore, the one and only way to deal with this kind of sin is to be open and direct, and that was exactly how Zechariah dealt with this contingent.

We all know what happened to Zechariah for calling their hand. Sure, Jesus tells us in Matthew 23:35: "…unto the blood of Zechariahs, son of Barachias, whom ye slew between the temple and the alter." Yes, these from Babylon ended up killing Zechariah right there in the newly built temple, because Zechariah spoke the truth to them: (We know they didn't do it then and there on the spot, because Zechariah made several prophecies after this time. He was killed several years later. Nevertheless, it was church people that killed him).

Church, please hear these words of Zechariah, chapter seven: For we too are about God's business, and God is no less serious than he was in Zechariah's day. Church, please do not "Stop your ears that you should not hear" (Zech.7:11).

Now that we are coming to the completion of the church age, so many pious church goers are coming forward to stand in the limelight. They are coming without faith, true faith. They talk and act like Christians on the outside, but inside they are as the Babylonian contingent, faithless.

In itself, being faithless wasn't what betrayed them. In fact, we all have these times of faithlessness. No, the real problem was that the faithless ones, "…stopped their ears that they should not hear" (Zech.7:11).

Are you suggesting we are faithless?

Let me explain, but first we need to take a short look at Zechariah 7.

> *… they had sent unto the house of God Sherezer and Regemmelech, and their men, to pray before the Lord, and to speak unto the priests which were in the house of the Lord of hosts, and to the prophets, saying, Should I weep in the fifth month, separating myself, as I have done these so many years? Then came the word of the Lord of hosts unto me, saying, Speak unto all the people of the land, and to the priests, saying, When ye fasted and mourned in the fifth and seventh month, even those seventy years, did ye at all fast unto me, even to me? And when ye did eat, and when ye did drink, did not ye eat for yourselves, and drink for yourselves?... And the word of the Lord came unto Zechariah, saying, Thus speaketh the Lord of hosts, saying, Execute true judgment and shew mercy and compassion every man to his brother: And oppress not the widow, not the fatherless, the stranger, not the poor; and let none of you imagine evil against his brother in your heart. But they refused to hearken, and pulled away the shoulder, and stopped their ears, that they should not hear. Yea, they made their hearts as an adamant stone, lest they should hear the law, and the words which the Lord of hosts hath sent in his Spirit…*
>
> *Zechariah 7:2-6, 8-12*

This contingent comes two years after Zechariah made his earlier seven fold prophecies. All of which were positive and uplifting good news for Israel. Probably, that was how long it took for word to filter back to Babylon; get the faithless ones attention; and organize a contingent to go up to Jerusalem to see if all this was true.

OK, here comes this group, and they have come for a noble cause (or so they thought), "to pray before the Lord" (Zech.7-2). If they had done that and just that, then maybe their trip might have been profitable. However, that wasn't their true motive for coming. (Zechariah tells us later on what their true motive was, and Jesus in Matthew testifies to the validity of Zechariah's words on the matter). They stated further that they had come, "…to speak unto the priests that were in the house of the Lord of hosts, and to the prophets…" (Zech.7:3).

Here again, if this was their true desire, they would have spoken; heard the prophet's reply; and maybe, just maybe, they would have taken those words to heart, and humbled themselves, and then pitch in to help the faithful. However, speaking to the priests and prophets wasn't their true desire. To the contrary, they wanted to show how pious they were, or thought they were. They asked, "…should I weep in the fifth month, separating myself, as I have done these so many years" (Zech.7:3)?

Oh yuck! By this time, even the least of the Jerusalem faithful could tell these guys were phonies. They opened themselves up to Zechariah. Stand back, because Zechariah is going to expose their sin of propriety for all to see:

> *Then came the word of the Lord of hosts unto me, saying, Speak*
> *unto all the people of the land, and to the priests, saying, when*
> *ye fasted and mourned in the fifth and seventh month, even those*
> *seventy years, did ye at all fast unto me, even to me?*
> *Zechariah 7:4, 5*

At first glance, their question seems much in order. After all, they were dealing with a real spiritual issue here, or so they tried to make Zechariah believe, but he wasn't having any part of it.

They were asking, now that the temple was all but finished does that mean we won't have to fast the tenth day of the fifth month, which commemorated the day King Nebuchadnezzar burned the temple and city some seventy years ago? In other words, they wanted to know if the significance for the fast was gone now that the temple was rebuilt. Their prayers for those many long years were now answered.

Oh, what nice guys, they have come to see the answer to their prayers. Whoopee, now we don't have to pray anymore. As if it was their prayers that moved God in the first place.

We see a similar situation in the Gospel of Luke:

> *And it came to pass, that, as they went in the way, a certain man*
> *said unto him, Lord, I will follow thee whithersoever thou goest.*
> *And Jesus said into him, foxes have holes, and birds of the air*
> *have nests; but the son of man hath not where to lay his head.*
> *And he said unto another, follow me, but he said, Lord suffer me*
> *first to go and bury my father. Jesus said unto him, let the dead*
> *bury their dead:*
> *Luke 9:57-60*

Jesus accepts the request from the first man, but a second man, a disciple, (In Matthews account the second man is a disciple: Matthew 8:18-22) immediately says that he needs to look after some important matters first. To go and bury one's father sounds like a reasonable request, but that is exactly what is at issue here. Please see this dear brothers and sisters: Even the best excuse is no excuse when it comes to serving our Lord. If the Lord is not all in all, then he is nothing at all. To serve the Lord is to serve him with no reservations; even good reservations. Nevertheless, the disciple gave an excuse, and a good one at that. Even Jesus would understand.

Wrong! Just as Zechariah saw through the pretenses of those from Babylon; Jesus saw through this man's propriety (goodness). On the surface, it looks as if Jesus is harsh and insensitive towards the scribe, but the scribe was a fake. Jesus saw through him, and exposed the man for who he was. You see, the Matthew account tells us that "great multitudes" were about the Lord. This was at the beginning of the Lord's public ministry, and the crowds were now gathering and following Jesus. It was only natural to want to be a part of this new ministry. After all, if this second man played it just right he might get in on the ground floor, and ride this new prophet's coat tails to prominence. However, Jesus nipped that notion in the bud quickly, "Let the dead bury their dead."

When a ministry begins to take off many want to be a part of it. That is what was taking place in Jerusalem that day in Zechariah chapter seven. For years it looked as if the temple would never be rebuilt. You couldn't get anyone to leave the comforts of slavery in Babylon to help out. Only a fool would go to Jerusalem to fight the elements, the harsh living conditions, the opposition, and most of all the jokes. For years the prophets in Jerusalem were laughed at, but now, not only was the temple rebuilt but Jerusalem, the city, was taking shape. It was fast becoming apparent to even the non-Jews that God was indeed alive and well in Jerusalem. Now, everyone wanted to be a part of this. Yet, where were these guys when Zechariah needed them. Now that the temple was all but finished, they show up; and Zechariah let them know about it too. Jesus, likewise, saw through the disciples' façade, and Jesus called it for what it was: "No man, having put his hand to the plough, and looking back, is fit for the kingdom of God" (Luke 9:62).

Dear brother and sister, it may seem harsh and insensitive to tell someone to, "Let the dead bury the dead." Likewise, it may seem harsh and insensitive to tell you gals to submit, and you guys to get serious, and prove yourselves with actions and not words, for God's business is serious business. Only drastic change will get you on board, because God is right now finishing things up here on this earth. Don't wait until the third temple is finished before you show up to help, or you will be found to be in opposition to God. (The temple Zechariah built was the second temple. That temple was later destroyed by the Romans, and is presently waiting to be rebuilt for the third and final time).

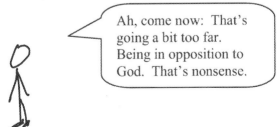

Ah, come now: That's going a bit too far. Being in opposition to God. That's nonsense.

You think that sounds harsh. Take a look at the word of God more closely: "He that is not with me is against me; and he that gathereth not with me scattereth abroad" (Matthew 12:30). Who do you suppose opposed God by killing Zechariah, "between the temple and the alter?"

It was the people of God that killed the people of God (Matthew 23:34, 35). It was the Old Testament church that killed the Old Testament prophets: "O Jerusalem, Jerusalem, thou that killest the prophets, and stonest them which are sent unto thee," (Matthew 23:37). And dear brother and sister, who do you, suppose will be the ones that will oppose God in this day? Who do you suppose will persecute the saints of the New Testament? Come now, dear Christian, let's not be naïve. Why don't you pull your head out of that TV so you can see what is really going on. You think it is the government that will do all the persecuting of the New Testament saints. Sorry, that is not so. No, dear Christian, the ones that will be in opposition to God, and who will be doing the persecution are to be found in those pews and behind those pulpits each Sunday.

Take a look at history, especially the last 1700 years. You will see that it was the church itself that persecuted the men and women of God. Oh, the governments were involved, but those behind the pulpits and in the pews did the dirty work. Liberal or conservative, they are all involved. In fact, the more "good" and "right" they are the more they will be involved in the persecution.

How about you gals? Have you, "pulled away your shoulder and stopped your ears...", or are you still upset about things not being fair?

I hope you are beginning to see that this thing of God being fair or not fair is really a non-issue. Hopefully, what begins to surface is God himself, the very person of God. After all, this is the ultimate issue.

How about you guys?

Guys, I hope a sense of urgency is beginning to creep into your lives: the urgency to get closer and closer to our loving Father. This is where Job comes in.

CHAPTER FOUR

THE MERCY OF HIS JUDGMENT

There are only two things we can receive from God, his mercy and his judgment (everything else he has already given us in Christ Jesus). His judgment he must give us. He is compelled to give us his judgment, for God is a just and holy God. That is what makes God to be God. Once God ceases from being a just God he then ceases to be God. So, God must give us judgment.

God does not have to give us mercy. If he never granted mercy to anyone, it wouldn't affect his status as God. However, we know that God does give us mercy. Again, understand he doesn't have to. How grateful we are that God is indeed a merciful God, but by all rights he doesn't owe anyone mercy. On the other hand, he does owe everyone judgment. In fact, there are times when God's judgment upon our lives is the most merciful thing he can do for us. Job understood this.

In Job 14:13, Job makes an astonishing statement: "O that thou wouldest hide me in the grave, that thou wouldest keep me secret, until thy wrath be past, that thou wouldest appoint me a set time, and remember me!"

Basically, what Job is saying is, I'd rather go to hell than face the judgment of God. In other words, hell is a picnic, even a place of rest compared to God's judgment.

Then Job turns right around and wants God to go ahead and do what is necessary to cleanse him: "Thou shalt call, and I will answer thee: thou wilt have a desire to the work of thine hands" (Job 14:15).

It sounds as if Job doesn't know his own mind. It looks as if Job is too caught up in his pain and suffering to think straight. However, that isn't the case at all. Dear brothers and sisters, Job is most sane. Job knows exactly what he is saying, and this right here is the very essence of the power found in the Christian faith.

Job realizes what the judgment of God is. Job understands 2 Corinthians 5:11: "Knowing therefore the terror of the Lord...". He knows that the judgment of God is so much worse than being in hell. In fact, hell is a reprieve, a retreat center, a pleasure compared to God's wrath. Thus, Job says, "hide me in the grave". However, no sooner had Job said what he said, he likewise knew that hell was not the answer to his problem.

> *If a man die, shall he live again? All the days of my appointed time will I
> wait, till my change come.*
>
> *Job 14:14*

After all, what will bring true happiness to a man? Sure, Job knew that we would only be happy when we were in fellowship with God. Thus, Job knew he needed to change, and hell could not produce that change. Only experiencing God's judgment upon his life would produce the change needed to grow ever closer to his Lord. Therefore, Job quickly changed his plea to the Lord. In affect, he said, Oh God, your wrath is worse than hell, but only this judgment upon a man can totally cleanse a man.

That is strange. Job was a righteous man already. God said so: "There is none like him in the earth, a perfect and an upright man, one that feareth God, and escheweth evil" (Job1:8).

What an endorsement, and this came from God's own mouth. Then what is it that Job still needed to change in his life? Please understand, this something was so terrible that hell itself could not cause the needed change in Job. This something was so bad only the judgment of God could cleanse Job of it.

Dear brothers and sisters, that something was the same something Zechariah said the nation Israel still had even after seventy years of exile. It is what the church today has so much of. That something is GOODNESS, or propriety, as Jean Guyon says (The Book of Job; Christian Book Pub., 1985). In other words, we are so good that it is slowly starving our relationship with the Lord.

Hell can not eradicate our goodness, and Job knew this and finally declared, Lord, do whatever it takes to cleanse me of this propriety:

> *Who can bring a clean thing out of an unclean? Not one...thou*
> *sewest up mine iniquity... thou washest away the things which*
> *grow out of the dust of the earth; and thou destroyest the hope*
> *of man. Thou prevailest...thou changest his countenance...*
> *Job 14:4, 17, 19, 20*

Job's love for the Father was so great that Job wanted nothing (including his goodness) to be between he and the Father, nothing.

Anything that comes between God and us is sin: Even if that something is good. Therefore, Job wanted that goodness to be cleansed from him as only God could do. We must understand that we in and of ourselves cannot eradicate goodness from ourselves. That would be using goodness to cleanse goodness. Only God can cleanse us! Consequently, let the judgment of God reign in our lives.

Paul writes of this same thing in his letters to the churches in Corinth:

> *For we must all appear before the judgment seat of Christ; that*
> *every one may receive the things done in his body, according to*
> *that he hath done, whether it be good or bad. Knowing therefore*
> *the terror of the Lord, we persuade men; but we are made manifest*
> *unto God; and I trust also are made manifest in your consciences...*
> *Wherefore henceforth know we no man after the flesh:*
> *II Corinthians 5:10, 11, 16*

Note: Paul was talking to Christians, mature Christians (At the time of his first letter to the Corinthians, they were anything but mature Christians. However, by the time Paul wrote the second letter the Corinthian church had come a long way). Likewise, Zechariah was dealing with mature church goers; and without question, Job was a mature saint. Yet, he too needed to change. In other words, we are dealing with the sin of goodness (propriety).

Now, look at how this sin must be dealt with. Paul calls the solution to this sin as, "knowing the terror of the Lord". Zechariah calls the solution to the sin of goodness as, "a great wrath from the Lord". Job refers to the cleansing of goodness as, "thy wrath". Yes, dear brothers and sisters, there is a time that God's judgment is actually his mercy. When judgment brings us into oneness (unity) with our beloved Savior that judgment is indeed sweet mercy.

Paul goes a step further in Romans, chapter eleven:

For if God spared not the natural branches, take heed lest he also
spare not thee. Behold therefore the goodness (mercy) and severity
(judgment) of God: On them which fell, severity; but toward thee,
goodness, if thou continue in his goodness: Otherwise thou also shalt
be cut off. And they also, if they abide not still in unbelief, shall be
grafted in: for God is able to graft them in again.

Romans 11:21-23

The Old Testament saints received God's judgment. The New Testament saints received God's mercy. However, there is a condition to his mercy, "if thou continue in his goodness" (Note: This is his goodness, not our goodness).

Paul is saying, lookout church, if God would do this to the Old Testament saints, he will do it to us. Do you think we are any better than they? Come now saints, God didn't save you because you were a good person.

We know that already. You don't need to lecture us.

Somebody needs to lecture, because we tend to forget, "…there is none that doeth good, no, not one" (Rom.3:12). We tend to forget that God doesn't owe us anything except his judgment, and just because he has given us mercy instead, doesn't mean he still won't give us his judgment. In fact, Paul tells the Corinthians that God's judgment is waiting for them even now: "For we all must appear before the judgment seat of Christ…" (2Cor.5:10).

What keeps us in his mercy? Sure, "if we continue in his goodness. Otherwise thou also shalt be cut off" (Rom.11:22).

Paul tells the Roman church after he walked them through salvation and deliverance. He tells us this only after we are mature in the faith. Likewise, when did Job experience the merciful judgment of God? Sure, after he was already, "perfect and an upright man" (Job 1:8). Consequently, the more mature need to be the most concerned about their relationship with our Lord. Paul put it this way:

I beseech you therefore brethren, by the mercies of God, that ye
present your bodies a living sacrifice, holy, acceptable unto God,
which is your reasonable service.

Romans 12:1

One way or the other we must be judged by God. Paul says for us to do it daily, and do it voluntarily, so the judgment can be sprinkled with God's mercy.

Peter put it this way:

Wherefore the rather, brethren, give diligence to make your calling
And election sure: for if ye do these things, ye shall never fall:

2Peter 1:10

What are these three, Job, Paul and Peter, telling us? They are saying: the most saved are the most concerned about their salvation. Those that are truly saved will never be satisfied with simply being saved. They will seek ways to prove to the Lord that they truly want to be with him, not only in the future, but in the here and now.

For the love of Christ constraineth us;...that they which live
should not henceforth live unto themselves, but unto him which
died for them...Wherefore henceforth know we no man after
the flesh:

2 Corinthians 5:14, 15, 16

However, we cannot in and of ourselves bring about the needed change. Flesh cannot overcome flesh. Consequently, we must present ourselves to God's hand of merciful judgment: thus the need for the oil press in our lives.

It is one thing to tell a drunk that he needs to shape up and get right with God. That is easy for everyone to see. However, to tell good church goers they need to change. Well, that is a whole different matter. Nevertheless, in the sight of God, our goodness is just as sinful as our badness. Come, dear Christian, let us follow the ultimate good person, Peter, as he experiences the oil press on his life.

CHAPTER FIVE

COMMITTED, DETERMINED AND ABLE

Something happened to Peter on the way to the cross. He fell asleep. After the Lord's supper, and on the way to the Mount of Olives, Jesus spoke to the disciples concerning his impending death:

> *All ye shall be offended because of me this night: For it is*
> *written I will smite the shepherd, and the sheep of the flock*
> *shall be scattered abroad.*
>
> *Matthew 26:31*

Peter retorted:

> *Peter answered and said unto him, though all men shall be*
> *offended because of thee, yet will I never be offended...*
> *though I should die with thee, yet will I not deny thee.*
>
> *Matthew 26:33, 34*

There is no question about it Peter meant every word he said. He was determined and totally committed to backing up these words with his actions. However, as we all know, Peter did the opposite. In fact, we know it was only a few hours later when Peter failed to live up to these words.

> *Now Peter sat without in the palace: and a damsel came unto*
> *him, saying, thou also wast with Jesus of Galilee. But he denied*
> *before them all, saying, I know not what thou sayest...again he*
> *denied with an oath, I do not know the man...and he went out,*
> *and wept bitterly.*
>
> *Matthew 26:69, 70, 72, 74, 75*

What a difference a few hours make. Hours before, there is this determined, positive warrior ready to take on the establishment. Two hours or so later he has turned into a pathetic wimp that runs from a lowly maid.

What caused the difference? Why couldn't Peter even partially fulfill his commitment?

One quick look at our Bible, and we can figure it out for ourselves: Peter slept thru the work of the oil press. Before the Garden of Gethsemane we had a confident, strong, and determined man of God. Immediately afterwards we have a cowardly, turn coat. This astonishing change took only one hour (between Matthew 26:35 and Matthew 26:56).

Now Christian, what does this convey to you? If Peter, upon which the church will be built (Matthew 16:18), crumbled within one hour: How about you and me? If Peter, who had committed his life to Jesus ("Then answered Peter and said unto him, behold, we have forsaken all, and followed thee; Matthew 19:27), in turn, forsook Jesus: How about you and me? If Peter, who walked step by step with our Lord, could so quickly run away from the very Son of God:

How about you and me? If Peter, who talked face to face with Jesus, could shortly thereafter deny he ever knew the man: How about you and me? If Peter needed to experience the working of the oil press upon his life: How about you and me?

Yes, dear Christian, the Garden of Gethsemane is essential to our walk. It is not a viable option to consider. Later on (2 Peter 1:10-15), Peter tells us repeatedly, without the oil press we too will fall. Not maybe fall: Not some will, and others won't: Peter says, you will fall; and of all people Peter should know.

Without the oil press working in us Peter says: "…he that lacketh these things is blind, and cannot see afar off, and hath forgotten that he was purged from his old sins" (2 Peter 1:9). In other words, it is as if we were never saved. Tell me, wasn't that exactly how Peter acted when he denied our Lord? Sure it was, and we aren't exempt. Read Peter's last words to the church in chapter one of 2 Peter. In fact, Peter tells us to be in a hurry about this oil press experience, "give diligence" (2 Peter 1:10).

What exactly is the oil press experience? What took place that hour in the Garden of Gethsemane? What is it we need, "that ye shall never fall"?

First, let's look at the people involved in the garden that evening: Of course, there were the three sleepy disciples. The central figure was Jesus, our Lord. We know God the Father is present, but there is still another person present. Yep, the devil was there also: "Watch and pray, that ye enter not into temptation" (Matthew 26:41). Absolutely, for this was the devil's finest hour; "…this is your hour, and the power of darkness" (Luke 22:53).

We also notice that Jesus prayed three times. He was near death. When he was finished, "an angel came and ministered unto him". Now, what does this look like?

No question about it; this is a rerun of the wilderness temptation. However, there are differences, as well as, similarities.

SIMILARITIES	DIFFERENCES
A. Jesus tempted three times	A. Wilderness temptation began Jesus' ministry; garden temptation was the end of his public ministry.
B. Jesus was near death.	B. Satan's presence wasn't obvious in the garden, whereas, he was the focus in the wilderness.
C. An angel came and ministered.	C. Temptations in the wilderness were extremely obvious, whereas, here in the garden the actual temptations were extremely difficult to discern.
	D. In the wilderness Jesus countered the temptations with the word of God: In the garden, prayer was used.

Doesn't it strike you as strange that the wilderness temptations were so obvious? They were extremely obvious! After all, Satan had known Jesus for thousands and thousands of years already. Both of them knew the scriptures backwards and forwards. In fact, it was the very

Spirit of Christ that wrote the Bible. Satan knew this fact, and Satan also knew he could have never deceived Jesus by misquoting the word of God. No, dear Christian, the three wilderness temptations were much too obvious to trip up the Lord. In fact, any twelve year old Hebrew boy would have known the answer to those three temptations in the wilderness that day. Then why, might we suppose, did Satan make those temptations so easy?

Could it be Satan never expected to defeat Jesus with those three feeble attempts? That had to be the case. Satan never expected, nor intended those wilderness temptations to foil the Lord. No, Satan presented those temptations; not to trip up Jesus, but to trip us up.

Yep, the church was the object of those temptations: Had to be, because Satan is no fool. No, he is extremely cleaver and doesn't waste his efforts; and one thing for sure about Satan: He is consistent.

To get at Adam, the devil went through Eve. Correct? Absolutely! He knew a direct attack against Adam would be futile. Likewise, Satan knew a direct attack against the Lord, the last Adam, would be just as useless. As Satan had to defeat the first Adam through the woman, Eve; so too, must Satan defeat Jesus by attacking his bride, the church. Yes, the wilderness temptations were for our benefit and ours only.

He did it that way so we, the bride, wouldn't notice the garden temptations. By our focusing on the wilderness temptations only, we are less likely to see what truly took place in the garden that evening. Secondly, Satan doesn't want us to use prayer. He would settle for us using just the word of God. You see, one without the other is vain and powerless. The word without prayer is not the word. Prayer without the word is not prayer. The two must go hand in hand to be of any use. To think otherwise is to be naïve and foolish. Without both prayer and the word of God equally hidden in our heart there can be no overcoming as the children of God.

He did. Don't you see; by making the wilderness temptations so very obvious, he actually concealed the true purpose of both temptations; and by our concentrating on only the obvious temptations, we wouldn't look any further. Therefore, with every encounter with the obvious wilderness type temptation, the less value we would place on prayer. Consequently, we would become a dysfunctional bride. So much so, that prayer would all but vanish from the lips of the church. Then, in the final hour, Satan will defeat us as Peter was defeated there in the Garden of Gethsemane.

He did. However, without prayer we are unable to perceive these temptations. Come now Christian, how many times did the Lord tell us about prayer? How often is prayer mentioned in the Bible? How many parables are about prayer? Let's be honest, dear Christian, prayer, real kingdom prayer, has become an unwanted yet tolerated step-child in our churches today. Therefore, it is no wonder we can't see the garden temptations. This was the very reason Peter fell so quickly. He slept rather than prayed: "watch and pray, that ye enter not into temptation:" (Matthew 26:41). Likewise, the church is sleeping, and like Peter, committed, determined and able, we too shall just as surely fall.

Something Andrew Murray wrote says it all:

> To the healthy, walking is a pleasure; to the sick, a burden, if not
> an impossibility (Andrew Murray; The Ministry of Intercession,
> Whitaker House; Springdale, PA 15144; 1982; p78).

In other words, Andrew Murray said the most natural thing for a healthy person is to walk. They enjoy walking. However, to a cripple the hardest task is to walk. Likewise, with a

Christian, the most natural thing is to pray. If prayer is a burden, then there is a disease present; pure and simple.

Can we now see this is what happened to Peter: "…Peter, What, could ye not watch with me one hour" (Matthew 26:40)? On the outside Peter came across as determined, committed, and with much ability. Spiritually he was a wimp. Oh church, we are so much like Peter. We want so much to please our Lord, but without the working of the oil press we too will be unable to, "watch one hour". Just as Peter had to experience the oil press so do we have to experience that same oil press. After all, Peter was emphatic about this:

> *Wherefore I will not be negligent to put you always in remembrance*
> *of these things,…that ye shall never fall.*
> *2 Peter 12:10*

CHAPTER SIX

WHICH CUP IS "THIS CUP"

To fully understand what Peter slept through that evening in, "a place called Gethsemane", we must first come to understand which cup is "this cup" referred to by Jesus in his prayer to the Father there in the Garden of Gethsemane: "O my Father, if it be possible, let this cup pass from me:…" (Matthew 26:39).

At first glance, it is naturally assumed that our Lord is referring to the cup of the cross. However, the more one reads this passage the more other scriptures come to light, all of which stand in stark opposition to the notion that "this cup" is the cup of the cross.

If "this cup" here in the garden refers to the cup of the cross, then how do we explain what Jesus told the disciples in Caesarea Philippi (Matthew 16:25)? At Caesarea Philippi, weeks prior to the cross, Jesus, "shew unto his disciples, how that he must go unto Jerusalem, and suffer many things of the elders and chief priests and scribes, and be killed…" Immediately, Peter sought to prevent Jesus from going to the cross. What was Jesus response?

As we might remember, Jesus gave Peter one of his sternest rebukes. He said to Peter, "…get thee behind me, Satan: thou art an offense unto me: for thou savourest not the things that be of God, but those that be of men" (Matthew 16:23).

Now, if here in the garden, just hours away from his previously declared destination, Jesus is asking the Father to, "let the cup (of the cross) pass from me…": isn't Jesus going directly counter to what he had said to Peter in Caesarea Philippi? Sure he is, that is if "this cup" of the garden is the cup of the cross; but it isn't.

Think about it. What kind of God would say one thing in Caesarea Philippi, and the very opposite in the Garden of Gethsemane? In the meantime, let us move to the Mount of Transfiguration in Luke, chapter nine. A few days after Jesus had finished rebuking Peter, Jesus is found on top of Mount Tabor; again, in the presence of Peter, James and John. This time Jesus is talking with Moses and Elijah and the topic of discussion is, "…his decease which he should accomplish at Jerusalem" (Luke 9:31). Of course, we know Jesus, Moses, and Elijah were talking about the cross, and all of this was done within the hearing of these three disciples.

Was Jesus so sure of himself in front of Moses and Elijah, yet weeks later in the garden at the eve of "his decease", he all of a sudden isn't so sure about what they discussed on Tabor? Come now, what kind of Savior is it that can plan his "decease" in one place, yet try to talk his way out of it when his time has come? Something doesn't make sense, that is, if "this cup" of the garden refers to the cross at Calvary: but it isn't.

Let us consider the next time the issue of the cross came up. This time Jesus and the disciples are even closer to the destination of the cross. They are, "…going up to Jerusalem" for the last time. Now, the group of them are only days away from the cross at Calvary, and, "then came to him the mother of Zebedee's children (James and John)…and desiring a certain thing of him…she saith unto him, grant that these my two sons may sit, the one on thy right hand, and the other on the left, in thy kingdom" (Matthew 20:20, 21).

We need to take special interest in Jesus' answer. He said, "…are ye able to drink of the cup that I shall drink of," (Matthew 20:22).

Compare that to Jesus' prayer to the Father in the garden, "O my Father, if it be possible, let this cup pass from me…" (Matthew 26:39).

No way can the cup on the way up to Jerusalem be the same as "this cup" in the Garden of Gethsemane. If they are the same then Jesus would simply be boasting and bragging to James and John's mother about something he wasn't willing to do himself. What kind of Lord is it that can be so positive one moment, but later doubt his very same words? In fact, the Holy Spirit rebukes this condition: "...if any man draw back, my soul shall have no pleasure in him" (Hebrew 10:38).

For Jesus to be Lord, Savior, and God incarnate, he could not ask the Father to "let pass" what he had told the son's of Zebedee he was going to drink himself. For God to be God he cannot lie, deceive or doubt.

No, dear Christian, the cup on the way up to Jerusalem was not, I repeat, was not the same cup Jesus referred to in his prayer to the Father in the Garden of Gethsemane.

One more reference will confirm this: During Jesus' last supper discourse to the disciples, Jesus emphasized and confirmed what had been said earlier in Caesarea Philippi, Mount of Transfiguration, and going up to Jerusalem. In Gospel of John, Jesus stated yet again in the most definite way possible that he indeed was destined for the cross. In fact, the essence for his coming is wrapped up in these following few verses:

> *Verily, verily, I say unto you, except a corn of wheat fall into the*
> *ground and die, it abideth alone: but if it die, it bringeth forth*
> *much fruit. He that loveth his life shall lose it; and he that hateth*
> *his life in this world shall keep it unto life eternal...Now is my*
> *soul troubled; and what shall I say? Father, save me from this*
> *hour: but for this cause came I unto this hour.*
> *John 12:24-27*

How could Jesus have uttered these words here, then only minutes later pray to the Father to, "...let this cup pass from me..."? That would be the actions of a double minded man, and we know what the Word of God says about that: "for he that wavereth is like a wave of the sea driven with the wind and tossed. For let not that man think that he shall receive anything of the Lord. A double minded man is unstable in all his ways" (James 1:6-8).

OK then, which cup is "this cup"?

Jesus tells us himself which cup "this cup" is when he says, "my soul is exceeding sorrowful, even unto death..." This is not an off hand comment, nor is it an exaggeration. Jesus was indeed near death right there in the garden. Luke, the doctor, confirms this fact: "and his sweat was as it were great drops of blood falling down to the ground" (Luke 22:44). It is my understanding this condition is a sure sign of impending death.

Jesus was indeed about to die right there, right then in the garden. It is this fact for which Jesus is referring to as "this cup". In essence, the Lord was asking the Father, 'Are you changing your plans? Have you decided to have me die right here, right now in the garden? Is there to be no cross after all? If that be the case, you have called off the cross, then, "O Father...not as I will, but as thou wilt". But, but Father, you know I want to go to the cross. I love my bride, the church, so very much. The cross is what I was destined for. But, O my Father, I love you even more, and my love for you comes first. Therefore, if you so desire for me to get so close, so very close to my goal, but you have now changed your mind; then so be it.'

Jesus' love for the Father meant more to him than salvation for us. He so loved us. Yet, he so loved the Father. If there had to be a choice between the Father and the church then Jesus' choice was for the Father; not his bride: "nevertheless not as I will, but as thou wilt" (Matthew 26:39).

Here in the Garden of Gethsemane Jesus reversed what was done in the Garden of Eden four thousand years earlier: When Eve gave the fruit of the forbidden tree to Adam, he had to make a monumental decision. If Adam had refused to eat of the fruit he would have lost Eve. She would then have been the only one to sin, and she alone would have been banned from the Garden of Eden. Adam would have God, but not Eve. If Adam ate of the fruit, he would have Eve, but not God. Thus, Adam had to choose between Eve, his bride, or God, his Father.

In the Garden of Gethsemane, Jesus had to make the same choice. If Christ died right there in the Garden of Gethsemane, and not gone to the cross; he would have God the Father, but he would not have had his bride, the church (For, as we learned earlier, the church came into existence at the cross: no cross, no bride). If Jesus refused "this cup" of the garden, like Adam, he would have his bride, but would lose the Father. Which would it be? Christ chose the Father over the bride: "nevertheless not as I will, but as thou wilt". Christ loved the church so much, but the love for the Father was greater; as it should be with you and me:

> *Thou shalt love the Lord thy God with all thy heart, and with all thy soul, and with all thy mind. This is the first and great commandment.*
>
> *Matthew 22:37, 38 & others*

The Garden of Gethsemane shows us that we serve a person not a purpose. God is a person, not a goal to attain. Therefore, effort, commitment, determination, and ability are of no avail; only obedience matters. When we strive to accomplish a goal, we need all these attributes. However, we serve a person, therefore, we need but one thing: loving obedience. That is all. There is no right or wrong. There is but one thing that matters, and that is Abba, Father.

Can we begin to see that right and wrong is indeed a non-issue for Christians? The only thing that matters is pleasing the loving Father.

God the Father had to make sure Jesus wasn't going to the cross for a good cause. There is one reason and one reason only for the cross; and that is in obedience to the Father. So it is with so many well meaning Christians when they attribute their "suffering" to that of the cross, whereas in reality, their pain comes from their struggle to advance right over wrong which has nothing to do with the cross. Sorry, before we can "suffer for Jesus" we must have the oil press do its work in our lives. We must have dealt with ourselves before we are ready for a ministry, and that means every drop of our goodness must be pressed out of us before we can go any further in our walk; even to the point of never again ministering for the Lord. In other words, every motive must be dealt with, regardless of how noble and pure we think it is. Are we following God for personal gain, however slight that may be, or do we follow our Lord strictly out of obedience? We won't truly know until we have gone to the garden to pray (a true inward lifestyle of prayer). It has to be inward prayer, because that is where our Lord is. He is not out there somewhere in the sky. He is within where soul meets spirit.

> *At that day ye shall know that I am in my Father, and ye in me,*
> *and I in you.*
>
> *John 14:20*

OK, let's look at why it is so very difficult to get past this point.

There is an eternally important reason Jesus had to go to the garden before he went to the cross. In fact, without the garden the cross would have been a failure. In fact, without the garden experience, our efforts actually benefit the devil. Yes, without the oil press we are actually found to be in opposition to God.

Tough words, but true nevertheless. In order to explain we will have to look at the "Battle for Calvary".

CHAPTER SEVEN

THE BATTLE FOR CALVARY

When Adam and Eve sinned that day in the Garden of Eden they did two things. First, they disobeyed God:

> *And the Lord God commanded the man, saying, of every*
> *tree of the garden thou mayest freely eat: But of the tree*
> *of the knowledge of good and evil, thou shalt not eat of it...*
> *Genesis 2:16, 17*

> *And when the woman saw that the tree*
> *was good for food, and that it was*
> *pleasant to the eyes, and a tree to be*
> *desired to make one wise, she took of*
> *the fruit thereof, and did eat, and*
> *gave also unto her husband with her;*
> *and he did eat.*
> *Genesis 3:6*

Secondly, they obeyed Satan:

How do you know they obeyed Satan?

Let me answer with a question. How did the devil come to be Prince of this world?

> *And the devil, taking him up into an high mountain, shewed*
> *unto him all the kingdoms of the world in a moment of time.*
> *And the devil said unto him, all this power will I give thee,*
> *and the glory of them: for that is delivered unto me; and to*
> *whomsoever I will I give it.*
> *Luke 4:5, 6*

Remember, God had given dominion of this planet to Adam, not Satan.

> *And God blessed them, and God said unto them, be fruitful,*
> *and multiply, and replenish the earth, and subdue it; and*
> *have dominion over the fish of the sea, and over the fowl of*
> *the air, and over every living thing that moveth upon the*

earth. And God said, behold, I have given you every herb
bearing seed,...every tree,...and to every beast of the earth,
and to every fowl of the air, and to every thing that creepeth
upon the earth, wherein there is life, ...and it was so.
Genesis 1:28-30

Seeing God made Adam boss of this planet: Seeing Adam had been given the title-deed to this planet: How did Satan end up with that deed? There is only one way Satan could have obtained title, and that is, Adam gave it to him.

Probably went something like this:

Thanks, Mister Serpent for being so kind as to show us how to get knowledge.

Yeah, Serpent, this knowledge stuff is really neat. We can on our own decide what is best for us.

Now we don't have to go through our Lord for every little thing. We can decide for ourselves what is good. In appreciation of our independence from God, we gladly give to you this title-deed to this planet.

That was stupid of Adam and Eve, ugh? It sure was, yet we continue to do the same thing time and time again in the here and now. Sure we do. How much does the church do today because it is "the right thing" to do verses "the wrong thing"?

We serve a person not an event. God is a live person, not a goal to be attained. Christians should never ask, "What is the right thing to do?" Our only question should be, "What does the Lord want?" Let me explain why, "The right thing is the wrong thing to do". Please don't, "Pull away your shoulder and stop your ears, that you should not hear" (Zechariah 7:11).

Adam and Eve did two things that day in the Garden of Eden: they disobeyed God, and obeyed the devil. Thus two consequences occurred:

<u>Consequence for disobedience to God:</u> Man had now sinned. Thus, God was compelled to ban Adam and Eve from his presence. A holy God and sinful man can not exist together. Holiness and sin cannot be in the same place at the same time. One of them must go. For God to remain God, he must remain holy. Therefore, his holiness would consume a sinful Adam and Eve ("For our God is a consuming fire"; Hebrew 12:29). Consequently, God banned the two from his presence. Another reason was the tree of life. In their sinful state God could not have them partake of the tree of life or else they would have lived forever in their sin. That would have been hell on earth. Think about it: Live thousands and thousands of years, but can't die. World greatly overpopulated; can't die. Not enough food and everyone starving but can't die. Have cancer and not able to die. Aged and feeble; still can't die. Thirsty, yet can't die. Air totally polluted with no clean air and unable to breath yet can't die. In auto accident after auto accident with every bone in the body broken; still can't die. Death longed for but still can't die.

So he drove out the man; and he placed at the east of the garden
of Eden Cherubims, and a flaming sword which turned every way,
to keep the way of the tree of life.

Genesis 3:24

Why did God have to put the tree of knowledge in the Garden in the first place?

When God created man he didn't want man to be just a robot. God made Adam and Eve with a free will. Ninety nine percent free is not free. Therefore, to be truly free man had to be one hundred percent free. Therefore, to give Adam and Eve complete freedom; God had to give them the freedom to reject the very one that gave them that freedom. Also, God had to give Adam and Eve something to choose between. However, this something had to be something good and of value. It wouldn't be much of a choice if man had to choose between God and bubble gum. Consequently, God placed the tree of knowledge in the Garden of Eden, and forbade them from eating of it so Adam and Eve would have something of great value to choose in place of God. For Eve, to choose between God and the tree of, "knowledge of good and evil" was a fair choice. Not only was the tree "to be desired to make one wise", the fruit was "good for food" and was also "pleasant to the eyes". Eve freely chose knowledge, goodness and beauty and ate of the tree. For Adam, he was given a choice between God and Eve. Adam freely chose Eve. In their disobedience, they both became free from God, thus, sin and death were born that day in the Garden of Eden.

Consequence for obedience to Satan: Because Adam and Eve obeyed Satan, they became Satan's servant/slaves.

Know ye not, that to whom ye yield yourselves servants to obey,
his servants ye are to whom ye obey;

Romans 6:16

God's people were in a pickle: They were banned from the presence of God, and bound to the devil. However, God had a plan for his people, and we all know what that plan was.

Sure, Jesus was that plan.

That is partially true. The plan God devised to bring his people back to himself was the law: the law of right over wrong; of good and evil.

Wait a minute. All along you tell us not to think in terms of right and wrong. Now you're changing things. What gives?

Hear me out. Please don't, "stop your ears that you should not hear" (Zechariah 7:11). I say it again. The plan of redemption was the law. In fact, the law was holy.

> *Wherefore the law is holy, and the commandment holy, and*
> *just, and good.*
>
> *Romans 7:12*

To bring his people back to himself, God gave a holy righteous law. By a sinful people fulfilling the holy law in their lives, they in turn become righteous. Therefore, a righteous holy people can then come back into the presence of a holy God.

But, but we can't obey the law.

That doesn't mean God abandoned his plan for a holy law as the way back to him: "…one jot or one tittle shall in no wise pass from the law,…" (Matthew 5:18). God knew we couldn't obey the law, but the people of God didn't know that. They had to find out by day to day experience. In fact, this is the Old Testament story to us today:

Hey, we couldn't do it, and you New Testament saints can't do it either. We all need someone who can.

Not only was the law holy; it was a curse as well. To come back to a holy God we had to fulfill the holy law. However, not to fulfill the law was to bring the curse of the law upon us.

> *For as many as are of the works of the law are under the curse:*
> *for it is written, Cursed is every one that continueth not in all*
> *things which are written in the book of the law to do them`.*
>
> *Galatians 3:10*

What Adam and Eve did that day in the Garden of Eden was devastating to all of us. The only way back to a holy God could only be done by each of us fulfilling the law. We all are unable to do this therefore we are all under the curse of that same law. In addition, we are each bound to Satan as the one, "...that had the power of death, that is, the devil;..." (Hebrews 2:14).

Now, you've got it. God knew all along we would never be able to fulfill the law, so he sent someone to do it for us, his Son! Thus, righteousness is imputed to us by faith through the Son's fulfilling of the law:

For as by one man's disobedience (Adam) many were made sinners,
so by the obedience of one (Christ) shall many be made righteous.
Romans 5:19

At the same time on the cross Christ redeemed us from the curse of the law:

Christ hath redeemed us from the curse of the law, being made a
curse for us: for it is written, Cursed is every one that hangeth
on a tree.
Galatians 3:13

Because Jesus, God the Son, did it all; fulfilled the law, we don't have to obey the Ten Commandments. All we have to do is obey him.

At first, it appears as if there is a fine line between the two, the law or the Lord. However, there is a vast difference: thus, the need for prayer, a lifestyle of prayer. To discern the difference between obeying the law and obeying the Lord takes a mature inward prayer life. Over and over again, we seek to follow our Lord when in fact we are doing good against evil and right over wrong. Sounds a lot like Paul:

For that which I do I allow not: for what I would, that do I
not; but what I hate, that do I ... For the good that I would
I do not: but the evil which I would not, that I do...O wretched
man that I am! Who shall deliver me from the body of this death?
Romans 7:15, 19, 24

How do we get out of this rut? The answer is simple… position, not performance. Paul is saying, we must quit performing and assume our proper position.

And what might that be?

We must die. Actually, we are already dead: that is, if we are saved.

> *Know ye not, that so many of us as were baptized in Jesus Christ were baptized into his death?...we have been planted together in the likeness of his death.*
>
> *Romans 6:3, 5*

God established the law as the way back to him. The law was holy and would never go away. However, we could never obey that law. This is what Paul was having so much trouble with in Romans 7:15-24. If we are wed to a husband (law, and holy at that); then, "…the law hath dominion…" (7:1). "For the woman (church) which hath a husband (law) is bound… to her husband as long as he liveth;" (7:2). And we know that the law will always be. It will never disappear (Matthew 5:18). At the same time, however, we can never satisfy the demands of our husband (law). How can we get back to God? "Who shall deliver me…?" (7:24).

What do we do? We can't divorce our husband (law), and go to Jesus, because that would be adultery: "So then if, while her husband (law) liveth, she be married to another man (Christ), she shall be called an adulteress" (7:3).

What do we do? We don't do anything! We simply assume our proper position, death. If we (the woman) die, then she is free from her first husband (law). Once she is free from the law (husband), she, at that point is free to obey another man (Christ).

Therefore, the key to the resurrected life is position, not performance. To get back to God, we don't have to "do" anything. All we have to do is assume our rightful position.

> *For if we have been planted together in the likeness of his death,*
> *we shall be also in the likeness of his resurrection:*
>
> *Romans 6:5*

> *And if we be dead with Christ,… we shall also live with him.*
>
> *Romans 6:8*

Now that we are, "dead unto sin but alive unto God through Jesus Christ our Lord" (6:11); we are to obey our Lord, not the law. At this place of death to our flesh in this world, "There is therefore now no condemnation to them which are in Christ Jesus,…" (8:1): Once in this position (death of our flesh) we are free to, "walk after the Spirit" (8:1).

It was in the garden (Eden) we lost fellowship with our Father, and it is in the garden (Gethsemane) that we regain access to our Father. In the first garden we preferred performance (being right and good) to the person of the Father. It is in the last garden where we lay down our goodness and rightness for our loving Abba, Father.

After the encounter in the garden, our Lord then went victoriously to the cross and:

> *Blotting out the handwriting of ordinances that was against us,*
> *which was contrary to us, and took it out of the way, nailing it*
> *to his cross.*
>
> *Colossians 2:14*

Jesus also accomplished another thing that day on the cross:

> *And having spoiled principalities and powers, he made a shew*
> *of them openly, triumphing over them in it.*
>
> *Colossians 2:15*

(Please see addendum I; p.91)

CHAPTER EIGHT

GOD'S PLAN, THE PERFECT SUBSTITUTION

Previously, we dealt with Adam and Eve's disobedience to God, and the consequences that resulted. Now, we will deal with Adam and Eve's obedience to the devil, and the resulting consequences.

Remember, that eventful day in the Garden of Eden when Adam and Eve did two things: One, they disobeyed God; and secondly, they obeyed the devil. There was not one act. They did two distinct things that day. Therefore, two distinct victories had to be won at the cross on Calvary to reverse those two actions. In the last chapter, we detailed the first:

> *Blotting out the handwriting of ordinances that was against us,*
> *and took it out of the way, nailing it to the cross.*
> *Colossians 2:14*

This chapter we will discuss the second aspect of the victory of the cross:

> *And having spoiled principalities and powers, he made a shew*
> *of them openly, triumphing over them in it.*
> *Colossians 2:15*

Not only is God a holy God; he is a just God. The fulfillment of the law by Jesus Christ satisfied a holy God. Now, a just God has to be satisfied. Jesus accomplished both upon the cross (Colossians 2:14 and 15).

For God to remain God, he must administer the same punishment for the same crime, or else he is not just. Therefore, God must see that those that committed the same crime must receive the same sentence (punishment). He cannot give one life in prison, and let the others go free.

Back there in the Garden of Eden, when Adam and Eve obeyed the devil, they, at that point, became accomplices to Satan and his crimes. Consequently, all those that follow are in league with Satan too, because we are in affect Adam and Eve in the present tense. We stand in their place. Therefore, we too must receive the same judgment upon our lives as does Satan. God is compelled to do so, or else he ceases to be God.

You might say that isn't fair. You weren't the one that sinned. It was our grand parents, Adam and Eve, not you. However, we forget, God did not have to let Adam and Eve live past the very second they obeyed the devil. By all rights, God could have killed (passed judgment) those two then and there. However, he showed them mercy by withholding that judgment. Because of the time delay Adam and Eve have become the human race of today. Thus, placing judgment on us today is in affect placing judgment on Adam and Eve. Therefore, God is compelled to sentence each of us to hell along with Satan, or else he can no longer be God. God is more than fair. He has withheld judgment for some six thousand years now. He has given each of us time to get right with him. However, the day is fast approaching when God will no longer withhold his hand of judgment from the human race. (1)

The love God has for us could not sway his judgment of us. Don't you know, Satan and all his devilish cohorts are going to pay particular attention to this detail?

Hate to disappoint you guys, but God can not let Satan and his demons go free, because that too would disqualify God as a just God. Rebellion and sin must be punished. What kind of judge would completely over look a crime, and let the perpetrators go scot-free? Therefore, for God to be a just God he must punish sinners. He must, or else he is no longer God. Consequently, the whole human race had a death penalty imposed against it on the very day Adam and Eve disobeyed God, and in turn obeyed the devil. We along with Satan were doomed to hell. We were to be cell mates with the devil.

Satan wasn't too worried, because the devil knew God would never do it. Satan knew that God would keep putting off the actual sentence of damnation, because God loved us so.

Meanwhile in heaven, all the angels are puzzled. God is compelled by his very nature to administer judgment upon his bride to be as well as upon Satan. It appeared as if God was trapped by his very own nature, or was he?

GOD'S PLAN: The law stated that someone could substitute for a convicted criminal. That is, if certain qualifications were met. If the right person could be found then the criminal could go free. That is, as long as the substitute served the full sentence. Also, justice was served as long as proper punishment was administered. However, there were two qualifications that must be met before a substitution could take place: Number one, the substitute must be of the same family or blood line as the convicted criminal. Secondly, the substitute must be a worthy substitute (That prevents a convicted criminal from paying some street bum to take his place).

The establishment of that law started at the beginning of the Old Testament, and goes to the end. That, my friends, is the major theme that runs through the entire Old Testament.

Abel pointed to the necessity of the lamb as a substitute for his father and mother's disobedience to God, and obedience to the devil. Abraham witnessed to the fact that God, himself, would provide the necessary lamb. Other words, the substituted lamb would not require our "doing" anything. God would do the doings. All we, like Abraham, needed to do was walk by faith in obedience to God.

Moses and the Passover lamb showed to all God's people the necessary lamb must die. Die as a substitute for the people of God. The blood of the lamb would be used in place of the people's blood. The lamb must die, that God's people could go free.

The Book of Leviticus shows us that the substituted lamb was going to be a divine lamb, "a lamb without blemish". Yes, the lamb was going to be a worthy lamb indeed. The lamb would be God.

The prophets gave the special identifications and characteristics of that substituted lamb. In fact, there were some four hundred fifty six prophecies detailing the identification of the lamb (The Life and Times of Jesus The Messiah, by Alfred Edersheim; Book 3, 1971; p710 ff).

Then there was provided a prophet of prophets to introduce the substituted lamb to the bride. The prophet's name was none other than John the Baptist.

Yes, dear friends, how could anyone possibly miss the law of substitution found in God's word? It runs from cover to cover in the Bible. The law of substitution wasn't some obscure law put in at the last moment. No, the substitute lamb is the very foundation of the law (The Master Theme of the Bible, by J. Sidlow Baxter; Tyndale, 1973).

An example would be the case of the fifty-two hostages held captive in Iran for four hundred and forty four days back in the late seventies.

Mohammed Ali volunteered to take the fifty-two hostages' place. However, he was politely turned down by the Iranians. Why? Mohammed Ali was a great boxer. He was a "good" man, and had good intentions. Nevertheless, despite these good qualities, he wasn't worthy enough to substitute for all fifty-two hostages.

If the Premier of Russia had volunteered to take the place of the fifty-two hostages (of course, he never did), he too would have been turned down by the Iranians. Again, why? After all, he was worthy enough.

Being the number one man from such a big and powerful nation certainly would qualify him to be worthy enough to take the hostages' place, however, the Premier of Russia wasn't from the same bloodline (heritage) as the hostages. The hostages were American. He was

Russian, and the Iranians had no beef with the Russians. Therefore, a head of state was worthy enough, but had to be of the same blood-line.

On the other hand, if Jimmy Carter, the President of the United States at the time of the hostage crisis, had volunteered to take the hostages' place, the Iranians would have leaped at the chance to make the switch. He was both worthy and from the same bloodline. In fact, having Jimmy Carter as a hostage would have suited the Iranians more, much more, than fifty-two regular hostages.

If President Carter had taken the hostages' place, the Iranians would have bound Carter, beaten him, and paraded him all up and down the streets of Teheran for the world to ridicule him. Then they would have spit on him, possibly hung him from a tree, and finally would have killed him. (2)

One for fifty-two does meet the demands of justice. That is, if the one is worthy and of the same bloodline. Now, to find someone that could qualify to take the people of God's place.

God had the solution. He would be the substitute. God would take the bride's place. No question about it, God was the one person worthy enough to substitute for so many, but he had to be kin, or of the same bloodline: Thus, the absolute necessity for the virgin birth. Jesus Christ, as God would be born of the "seed of woman", yet fathered by the Holy Ghost. That way he would be divine, worthy, and at the same time human, same bloodline (heritage). Therefore, the two qualifications of substitution for a convicted criminal, the bride, would be met. (3)

Jesus, the God/man, was fully divine and fully human. He was not part divine and part man. He had to meet both qualifications completely. Just as Jimmy Carter, if he had substituted for the hostages, would not have been part president or part American. He was fully both. Likewise, Jesus Christ was fully God and fully man.

---

(1)   There are two judgments from God: One is a judgment on who we are as seen here in this chapter; the other on our life as found in the Book of Job (chapter four).

(2)   Please understand, this is an illustration, and all illustrations have their limitations, and the limitation in this case is that God is the one who needs to be satisfied, not the devil. This illustration might lead us to think that the devil is the one holding us accountable (Not hostage, because God doesn't operate that way). Also, the emphasis of this illustration is not on the fifty-two hostages, but on the substitute for the fifty-two.

(3)   That's right, we, at birth were destined for hell. It is only the grace of God that saves us from hell. The word save is a fishing term. As the fisherman draws in his net, he separates the fish. Those fish he doesn't want, he throws back into the deep (hell). The others, he keeps, "saves", as his own (again see Volume III).

CHAPTER NINE

SATAN'S PLAN, STOP HIM

God's plan was set in motion. However, Satan wasn't sitting around, because he knew if the bride became free, then God would move swiftly against him and his demons.

Yes, Satan set into motion a plan to counter God's plan. It was simple: keep the God/man off that cross.

First, Satan would do everything possible to prevent the God/man from coming to this earth to take on the bloodline of the bride. Jesus was already divine. Satan couldn't stop that, but he could prevent the other. However, time after time, Satan's plan was foiled.

Abel walked by faith, thus Satan's first defeat. Next, Satan almost succeeded, but this time he again was narrowly defeated by another who walked by faith, Noah. The devil had influenced everyone on earth to follow after the things of this world, except one, Noah:

> *By faith Noah, being warned of God of things not seen as yet,*
> *moved with fear, prepared an ark to the saving of his house;*
> *by the which he condemned the world, and became heir of the*
> *righteousness which is by faith.*
>
> *Hebrews 11:7*

Then came Abraham; he claimed a land for the coming God/man. Isaac provided the coming savior with a lineage, a people. Jacob provided by faith a nation for the coming Messiah. Joseph preserved that nation. Moses gave the nation the holy law that would lead the people of God back to their Lord. Joshua united the nation with the land. David provided the earthly throne for the Son of God. By faith the prophets identified and characterized the coming Messiah. There were some four hundred and fifty six identifications of the God/man.

With so many characteristics no one would be able to miss the worthy one that would set God's people free from the bondage of sin. Then the best man, a prophet of prophets, was raised up to announce the coming groom for his bride.

The devil had failed to keep the Savior from coming. Now, he had to keep the God/man off the cross. To do that Satan would seek to disqualify the Christ. That called for a two fold attack. One, he would seek to disqualify Jesus as being worthy, fully divine. Secondly, the devil would seek to cause our Lord from being totally human.

If Satan could get Jesus to sin (disobey God the Father), then Jesus would no longer be fully divine (sin and holiness cannot exist together). Once the slightest sin existed, Jesus would not be found worthy to take our place. The other way to disqualify Jesus from being our substitute would be to get Jesus to use his divine powers for personal gain. Either way Satan would have thwarted God's plan of salvation for the church, his bride.

The devil didn't waste anytime. The wilderness temptations were a preview of things to come. The first wilderness temptation sought to get Jesus to use his own divine power for personal gain.

> *If thou be the Son of God, command that these stones be made*
> *bread.*
>
> *Matthew 4:3*

This is clearly something for personal gain.

> *But he answered and said, It is written, Man shall live by bread*
> *alone, but by every word that proceedeth out of the mouth of God.*
> *Matthew 4:4*

Next, the devil sought to get Jesus to disobey God. In this way Jesus would have no longer been fully divine.

> *Then the devil taketh him up into the holy city, and setteth him on*
> *a pinnacle of the temple. And saith unto him, If thou be the Son*
> *of God, cast thyself down: for it is written, He shall give his angles*
> *charge concerning thee: and in their hands they shall bear thee*
> *up, lest at any time thou dash thy foot against a stone. Jesus said*
> *unto him, It is written again, Thou shalt not tempt the Lord thy God.*
> *Matthew 4:5-7*

In the third temptation, the devil sought to get Jesus to make the same mistake the first Adam made: to obey the devil. In this way, the God/man would have been in bondage to the devil just as we were.

> *Again, the devil taketh him up into an exceeding high mountain,*
> *and sheweth him all the kingdoms of the world, and the glory of*
> *them; and sayeth unto him, All these things will I give thee, if*
> *thou will fall down and worship me.*
>
> *Matthew 4:8, 9*

As we know, Jesus wasn't fooled at all.

44

Then saith Jesus unto him, Get thee hence, Satan: for it is
written, Thou shalt worship the Lord thy God, and him only
shalt thou serve.

Matthew 4:10

The devil had now revealed his plan, and for the next forty two months Satan would have our Lord tempted in these two areas: To disqualify our Lord from being either fully divine (by disobeying God the Father); or disqualify our Lord from being fully human (by using his own divine powers for personal gain).

CHAPTER TEN

DELAY TACTICS

Weeks moved to months, and months to years. Satan was losing ground, and most of all, time. The God/man walked step by step closer to the cross on Calvary. If the God/man could reach the cross fully divine, and at the same time fully human, the bondage to sin will have been broken, and God's people through faith in Christ would again be righteous; thus having access to God the Father (That is, as long as we approach God the Father in Jesus Christ's name).

> *...to him that worketh not, but believeth on him that justifieth*
> *the ungodly, his faith is counted for righteousness.*
> *Romans 4:5*

The closer the God/man came to the cross the more pressure there was on Satan to stop him. Therefore, the devil stepped up his attacks upon Christ. Our Lord was attacked by politicians and government officials. Then there were the lawyers and social elite. However, the devil's most used and powerful weapon was the religious leaders, and at times, the devil even used the disciples against the Lord (Matthew 16:21-23).

Instead of stopping Jesus, each attack by the devil strengthened our Lord's advance towards victory on the cross. By Palm Sunday, it became ever increasingly apparent to all that Satan was losing the battle.

Four days from the cross went to three…; then two. Still, our Lord remained fully divine and fully man, his face steadfastly set towards the cross. Then came the night before the final day: What was Satan going to do? How was he going to keep the God/man off the cross?

There was only one thing to do: Continue to get the God/man to either disobey the Father, or use his divine powers for his own use. However, it just wasn't working. If the devil had failed for the past forty two months how was he going to succeed in the next forty eight hours?

Satan did a most unexpected thing: He quit! That's right, he quit fighting. He simply withdrew, conceded; gave up.

> *Then assembled together the chief priests, and the scribes, and*
> *the elders…and consulted that they might take Jesus by subtility,*
> *and kill him. But they said, not on the feast day.*
> *Matthew 26:3-5*

This was the same as saying, we give up. We are throwing in the towel. This was brilliant strategy, absolutely brilliant. Kill the God/man down the line somewhere, but not now. Let the Passover come and go. In this way all the prophecies would not be fulfilled. For Christ to be the Christ must die on the Passover.

All prophecy must be fulfilled for the law to be fulfilled. If any single prophecy wasn't fulfilled then due process would not have been satisfied. Without due process, there is no law. The two go hand in hand, law and prophecy (due process). Law without due process is not law.

Think not that I am come to destroy the law, or the prophets:
Matthew 5:17

The Old Testament consists of two major parts, law and due process (prophets). See Luke 16:29, 31; and Luke 24:27. Therefore, not one Old Testament prophecy could remain unfulfilled for due process to be achieved. Christ to be victorious had to die on Passover. The devil, by implementing stalling tactics at such a late hour had come up with an ingenious strategy. However, the Lord was way ahead of the devil. Look at the very next verse:

Now when Jesus was in Bethany, in the house of Simon the leper.
Matthew 26:6

At the very instant Satan and his cohorts were stalling in the city, the Lord was turning up the pressure two miles away in Bethany. [Please remember what took place those last forty eight hours just prior to the cross were involved and quite difficult to discern by mere observation. To understand the intricacies of those last few hours requires patience on the part of the reader. More importantly, to gain a good understanding, we must listen with our heart, not just our mind. We must also remember the God/man was not dealing with a fool. Satan was (is) an archangel. In fact, he was the angel of light. We are dealing with the two most intelligent minds in all of eternity, Jesus and Lucifer].

Jesus knew the Pharisees, on their own, were too cowardly to follow through with their threats. He knew they needed an advantage. The Lord also knew Judas needed the same. Therefore, Jesus gave them what they were looking for:

Then came unto him a woman having an alabaster box of very
precious ointment, and poured it on his head...
Matthew 26:7

As if that wasn't bad enough, the Lord commended the woman's actions. In fact, he gave her one of the highest commendations ever in the entire Bible.

Verily I say unto you, wheresoever this gospel shall be preached
in the whole world, there shall also this, that this woman hath
done, be told for a memorial of her.
Matthew 26:13

That did it! Judas couldn't handle anymore of this irresponsible handling of the finances. This woman wasted a whole year's wages, and the God/man thought it was a wonderful act. Enough is enough. Off he went to arrange the death of the God/man.

Then....Judas Iscariot, went unto the chief priests, and said unto
them what will you give me, and I will deliver him unto you?...
and from that time he sought opportunity to betray him.
Matthew 26:14-16

One down and one to go: Now to get the cowardly Pharisees to make a move.

Actually, Jesus had already been working on the scaredy-cat Pharisees ever since his entrance into Jerusalem on Palm Sunday. From sunup until sundown, the Lord had been teaching in the temple.

> *And in the day time he was teaching in the temple; and at*
> *night he went out, and abode in the mount that is called the*
> *Mount of Olives. And all the people came early in the morning*
> *to him in the temple, for to hear him.*
>
> *Luke 21:37, 38*

The God/man was in complete control of the city, especially the temple. This was simply great, that is, for everyone except the Pharisees.

> *Then gathered the chief priests and the Pharisees a council,*
> *and said, What do we? For this man doeth many miracles.*
> *If we let him thus alone, all men will believe on him: and the*
> *Romans shall come and take away both our place and nation.*
>
> *John 11:47-49*

It was common knowledge that those that occupied seats of power in countries controlled by the Roman Empire had to pay for those positions; and we are talking big bucks. Since Israel was an occupied nation, Caesar was the recipient of those payoffs. If Caesar didn't receive the prescribed amount from the high priest (in this case Caiaphas), then Caesar would have no more use for Caiaphas. Caesar would, therefore, order Pontius Pilate to get rid of the existing high priest and put someone else in that position; someone that would make the payments in a timely manner.

As long as the Lord was teaching in the temple, Caiaphas wasn't making any money. Passover was the time Caiaphas made the most money for the year, if not all his money. If he didn't make his payment to Caesar he was done for. (See addendum II; p. 94)

> *And one of them named Caiaphas, being the high priest that*
> *same year, said unto them, ye know nothing at all, nor consider*
> *that it is expedient for us that one man should die for the*
> *people, and that the whole nation perish not.*
>
> *John 11:49, 50*

In affect, Caiaphas was saying, let us cut the talk. Let us get serious here. It's my neck or his, and if you know what's good for you it will be that Jesus of Nazareth who dies, not me. If I go down I'm going to take everyone with me. No more need to be said.

> *Then from that day forth they took counsel together for to put*
> *him (Jesus) to death.*
>
> *John 11:53*

So much for Satan's delay tactics: The cross was on again. There was no stopping it now. There was too much momentum to turn it back now. The Lord had out maneuvered the devil. Now the devil was forced to make a move, and fast.

It was down to the last day. Less than twenty four hours remained. Satan had failed to keep the God/man from coming to this earth. He then failed to disqualify the God/man, and now his delay tactics were foiled. Yet, the devil remained determined.

OK, Jesus, you want to play hardball. You want to go to the cross…I'll see that you get there.

Then entered Satan into Judas, surnamed Iscariot…
Luke 22:3

CHAPTER ELEVEN

FACE TO FACE

...they made ready the Passover. Now when even was come, he sat down with the twelve. And as they did eat, he said, verily I say unto you, that one of you shall betray me.

Matthew 26:19-21

The God/man did a very unusual thing. He tipped his hand. He openly exposed Satan's plot. Jesus didn't have to do this. After all, everything was going the Lord's way, why press the issue? It simply wasn't necessary to bring up the subject. So then, why did he do this?

We are not told specifically why, but something Judas says later on sheds some light on the matter: After the Lord was arrested and in the hands of Pontius Pilate, Judas said, "...I have betrayed the innocent blood" (Matthew 27:4). In affect, Judas gave testimony that he could find no fault in Jesus. After walking with the God/man for forty two months (Remember, this testimony came from Satan's number one agent, his very own son: "...son of perdition"; John 17:12). What better proof could there be than having the prime witness for the prosecution testify that the God/man was indeed sinless. More than that, however, not only did the Lord fulfill the letter of the law, but he also fulfilled the spirit of the law. Why else would Judas give such an outstanding testimony for the accused? In fact, Judas returned the thirty pieces of silver. Why?

The reason Judas gave such a favorable report centers itself right here at the Passover meal. The Lord actually gave Judas an opportunity to repent and be saved when he said:

He that dippeth his hand with me in this dish, the same shall betray me.

Matthew 26:23

If Judas had any second thoughts, this would be the time he could simply not dip his hand into the dish. If Judas had declined, that would have served notice to all the other disciples that it was Judas who had planned to betray the Lord. His refusal to "dippeth" would have been evidence of his intent. Also, in refusing to "dippeth", he would be indicating he had repented, and wasn't going to go through with the betrayal after all. Besides, signaling he was the one, and he had now changed his mind, his refusal would also have dashed to pieces the Lord's plan of going to the cross on time. In other words, for the love of one man, the Lord would have given up the whole plan of salvation. Jesus was so concerned for Judas' soul he provided Judas with a perfect opportunity to repent and be saved. What love!

No wonder Judas was so torn. God loved him so much that he was willing to make Judas a child of God over and above winning the battle against the enemy. Jesus was willing to throw everything out for one soul, the soul of the son of the devil himself. Nevertheless, Judas passed up the opportunity to repent, and the "son of perdition" went to betray the Lord right on schedule.

Can't we see the vast implications here? Again the outcome of all eternity hung in the balance in those few seconds as Judas stood before the God/man. To foil the Son of God's plan, all Judas would have had to do was to refuse to go and betray the Lord: Just don't do it.

> *Verily I say unto you, one of you which eateth with me shall betray me. And they began to be sorrowful, and to say into him one by one, is it I?*
>
> *Mark 14:18, 19*

Sure, Judas would have been ostracized by the other eleven disciples, but the Lord's plan would have been defeated. The devil would have won, because prophecy would not have been fulfilled. If prophecy is not fulfilled then the law isn't fulfilled either, because of lack of due process.

However, we all know Judas "dippeth", and then went out to betray the God/man, thus prophecy was completely fulfilled.

> *...That scripture may be fulfilled, he that eateth bread with me hath lifted up his heel against me.*
>
> *John 13:18; Psalm 41:9*

Now, Judas had a real struggle. Here the Son of God had offered him an opportunity to repent and be saved, but Judas with his own free will refused the God/man to his face. Judas could never say he wasn't given a chance to be saved.

Yes, Judas had indeed betrayed innocent blood. For the Son of God had loved Judas just as much as anyone else, and again, the devil lost another confrontation with the God/man. Now, we go to the oil press.

CHAPTER TWELVE

VICTORY IN DEFEAT

Everything was going the Lord's way. Judas was off to finalize the betrayal. The Pharisees would gladly respond, despite the fact this meant the crucifixion would take place on the feast day (This put their plan at greater risk, but they were willing to take the chance. After all, their lives were at stake). Everything was on schedule. Then Jesus did a most unexpected thing: He retreated. He took a step backwards. He went outside the city walls. He crossed "over the brook Cedron"; up the Mount of Olives; and into the Garden of Gethsemane. The distance traveled was over a mile, but more significantly, it was late night. There were hundreds if not thousands of sleepy pilgrims along the way.

Although the Lord had done this many times before, doing it now was questionable, to say the least.

If Jesus had stayed in the upper room, he would have remained much more accessible to Judas and his, "band of men and officers from the chief priests and Pharisees..." (John 18:3). Also, by retreating to the Garden of Gethsemane, meant Judas would have to take all the men outside the city walls in the dark of the night with their, "lanterns and torches and weapons" (John 18:3). They couldn't help but wake up the entire country side of thousands of Passover pilgrims; possibly creating much confusion. Perhaps causing even a riot among the multitude (Remember, the multitude liked Jesus; at least for now. In twelve hours or so the multitude would turn against Jesus). Thus, by the Lord retreating in this way, he put the whole plan of salvation at great risk.

To fulfill prophecy he had to be off the cross and in the grave by sundown. By going outside the city walls meant there had to be perfect timing from this moment forward for due process to be satisfied. Nevertheless, Jesus had to find out from the Father if he was, in even the slightest way, going to the cross because it was the right thing to do. Had the Father changed his mind? Was this fully the Fathers' will? Jesus had to make sure, even at the expense of ruining the whole plan of salvation.

Oh Christian, this right here is the essence of our own salvation: loving God above all else. If our love for the Father is true all else will fall in place. God will see to that, just as he did with Jesus.

An additional problem resulted from the Lord going to the Garden. It provided the devil with one last opportunity to tempt Jesus. In fact, this would be the God/man's greatest temptation.

In the last forty eight hours Satan had retreated; "not on feast day". However, the Lord forced both Judas' hand and that of the Pharisees'; causing them to act from their own selfish motives: "better for him to die". Thus, the Lord foiled Satan's delay tactics. Then, when everything was completed, the God/man unexpectedly retreated to the Garden. Now, the devil was going to force Jesus to act on his own will power, thus breaking the unity between God the Father and God the Son.

All of Satan's temptations up to this point were designed to set up the God/man for this last hour in the Garden. Satan was going to get the last Adam to do exactly what he was able to get the first Adam to do: act independently from the Father. Satan wanted the Lord to go to the cross on his own will power. He wanted Jesus to do a good thing for a good cause. In other words, Satan sought to convince Jesus to do the right thing, at the right time, in the right place.

The devil brought Jesus to the point of death there in the Garden: "…even unto death…" (Matthew 26:38).

Jesus prayed to the Father.

Jesus prayed a second time to the Father.

A third time, Jesus prayed unto the Father.

The God/man remained subservient and obedient to the Father. He did not do the right thing, at the right time, in the right place. Jesus did not use his will power to overcome certain defeat. He waited until the Father said it was OK to go to the cross. The Lord had to make sure he and the Father were in perfect unity. This mattered more to the God/man than achieving his goal.

The Father did answer: "Then appeared an angel…" (Luke 22:43). The plan of salvation was on!

Once it was confirmed that the two of them, God the Father and God the Son, were in perfect unity, Jesus could then boldly say, "Rise, let us be going: behold, he is at hand that doth betray me" (Matthew 26:46).

Now, and only now, the God/man could "do" what he came to "do".

It would be twelve hours before the God/man had finished what he came to do; but let it be known Satan was defeated in the Garden before he was defeated on the cross. Likewise with us today: We must be in unity with the Lord before we can "do" for him. The obedience in the Garden must come before the sacrifice on the cross, and this requires prayer, a lifestyle of prayer.

All traces of our goodness must be pressed out of us before we can "do" for him. For, there can be nothing between us and the Father; not even what seems good. Only pure obedience experienced though the oil press can bring victory in defeat.

If Jesus had gone to the cross with the motive of doing something good he then would have gone as a man only. He would have died just as the two thieves died. There would have been no such thing as salvation. The cross would have been a victory for the devil, because Jesus would have done God the Father's will through God the Son's will. That, my friends, is sin, and any sin would disqualify Jesus from being divine, thus, no longer would Jesus have been worthy.

Can we see, in doing our thing, we are actually helping Satan do his thing? However, the Lord did not go to the cross on his own will power or commitment. Thanks to the oil press, the Lord went with God the Father's full approval. Therefore, Jesus won the victory. Satan had killed an innocent man.

When the God/man had taken his last breath, it was at that very moment Satan became a murderer (Up to that point, every other person had sinned, thus, deserving to die). Consequently, Satan lost all his rights to this planet (According to the law, murderers have no rights. Even today, criminals lose the right to vote etc.). Satan no longer was "Prince of this world" (John 12:31; John 14:30; John 16:11). Also, Satan lost the power of death over the human race.

> *...through death he might destroy him that had the power of death,*
> *that is, the devil.*
> *Hebrews 2:14*

Jesus now holds the title-deed to this planet.

> *...all power is given unto me in heaven and in earth.*
> *Matthew 28:18*

We now belong to Jesus Christ. Satan no longer has any rights in our lives. He lost all legal status once the God/man breathed his last. Satan is simply waiting to be sentenced. God is withholding that sentencing until all the harvest is in. Once the harvest is completed the time for grace will end and judgment will begin. In the meantime, Satan has one last hope: the bride. Actually, Satan never figured he could defeat the God/man. He has from the very beginning focused on the woman. First, it was Eve, the bride of the first Adam. Now, it is the bride of the last Adam, the church, that Satan is attempting to corrupt so there can never be a divine wedding. Believe it or not, the devil is using the very same tactics on the church as he used on Eve: And that is to get the church to do the right thing, at the right time, in the right place.

However, Satan is losing this last battle, thanks be to God. For, the end is near. The harvest is nearly in. Nevertheless, just as the devil saved the greatest temptations for the last hour against Jesus; so too, is he saving his greatest effort against us in these latter days.

Time is of essence. We have no time to waste.

> *And except those days should be shortened, there should no flesh*
> *be saved: but for the elect's sake those days shall be shortened.*
> *Matthew 24:22*

Bringing in the harvest is paramount and urgent. However, we must be careful in how we do it. After all, who is it that can corrupt the harvest the most? Sure, the labors in the fields can do the most damage to the harvest. Consequently, it is critical we "be" right before we can "do" right. Thus, is the need for the working of the oil press in our lives.

CHAPTER THIRTEEN

ME, MYSELF AND I

The Lord shows us in the garden how we can come to truly, "love the Lord thy God with all thy heart, and with all thy soul, and with all thy mind" (Matthew 22:37). So, let us take a look at the specifics to experiencing the oil press.

Jesus calls us to give up three things, all of which are "good". Nevertheless, they stand between us and the Father, and anything between us and the Father is bad, period.

Our identity is the first thing Jesus calls us to give up, "...terry ye here, and watch with me" (Matthew 26:38). Secondly, Jesus calls us to give up our will, "...not as I will, but as thou wilt" (Matthew 26:39). Finally, we are asked to relinquish our desires (or feelings), "...the spirit is willing, but the flesh is weak" (Matthew 26:41).

Did you notice that the three things we are to give up to God are the attributes of our soul? Our mind (identity), our will power (will), and our feelings (desires): These three things make up our soul.

When the, "perfect and ...upright", Job needed to change, this is what he was referring to (Job 14:14). Until we can relinquish these three parts of our lives, we can't stand against the enemy, nor can we get any closer to the Holy Ghost.

Now, don't go out and use your will power to erase your identity. You can't use your will to overcome the will. That is silly. You only strengthen your will when you seek to overcome by the will. Only God can do in you what needs to be done. You can't be determined to become undetermined. You can't be committed to become uncommitted. You can't desire to have no desires. No, dear brother and sister, our Lord simply calls, "..that ye present your bodies a living sacrifice, holy, acceptable" (Romans 12:1), and this is where prayer, a lifestyle of prayer, comes into play.

ME

Let's deal with the first aspect to the oil press working in our lives, our identity.

I don't like to bring this subject up again, but the issue of the TV has to be dealt with. It won't go away, because the TV does have a great influence upon us: a much greater influence than we would like to admit.

In the seventies an experiment was conducted where a person was fitted with a special pair of glasses. The glasses cause the wearer to see everything up side down. The floor is where the ceiling used to be, and the ceiling is on the floor. Even the most minor of tasks required assistance.

In the evening, the wearer would close his eyes, take off the glasses, and put on a blindfold for bed. In the morning he would reverse the order, making sure his eyes were closed until the glasses were in place.

After several days the wearer had learned to negotiate rather well with the upside down glasses. In fact, some tasks became fun to him.

On the forth day something strange happened. The wearer woke up, and as usual put the glasses in place then opened his eyes, and to his surprise everything had righted itself back to normal. The ceiling was where it was supposed to be, and the floor was at his feet again. The experiment was completed, so he took off the glasses, and behold, everything was upside down again: this time without glasses. Consequently, he had to go through the whole process all over again until several days later, he could see normally again.

The experiment was more than successful. It proved beyond a doubt that we truly see with our minds, not our eyes. It is the mind that decides whether something is upside down or not. It also shows that given enough stimuli the mind will accept the stimulus as true no matter how untrue it is. Up becomes down, and down becomes up. Most significantly, however, is the fact that the person themselves has no control over the process. The mind will do its thing independently from the wishes of the person. The person has no control, that is, if the mind can receive the same stimulus for long enough periods of time.

This right here is the major premise in which advertisers use in justifying spending billions of dollars to promote their products. They know given enough exposure, people will buy their products, even if the persons themselves don't like the product; even if the persons don't have the money to buy their product (They will borrow in order to buy). The advertisers know the mind works independently from the person. No wonder they will spend millions on just thirty seconds of advertising (In Super Bowl XLIV advertisers paid 2.4 million dollars for a thirty second ad). It works or else the business world wouldn't do it; and they aren't spending less each year for advertising. They spend more and more each year, because people are buying more and more each year. All because they are watching more and more TV year after year (In 2004 the TV in the average home was on for eight hours a day).

The saddest fact of all is that the people don't have the slightest idea what is happening to them. When asked people insist they are in control of their decisions. In fact, they get rather hostile over this issue. Another fact is that these misguided folks can not truly discern real from unreal until they have come out from under the influence of the TV for a significant length of time. So Christian, it's really fruitless to discuss your giving up your mind to God until you have been away from that TV for a long while, and the only way you will ever know I'm telling you the truth is to get rid of that TV (Simply turning the TV off doesn't work, you must get rid of it completely). Then and only then will you see that you have been under mind control all these years. Until then, you are completely unable to give your mind to God, because you have already given it over to the world.

MYSELF

Next, we cannot do God's will with our will. This is the essence of the garden experience. It is not enough to know what God's will is. We must do God's will with his power, not our commitment.

Right here is where many Christians get tripped up. They may identify with our Lord, yet there still isn't the Holy Ghost power present in their lives. They just can't figure it out. After all, they come to know what God's will for them is, but rather than wait; zoom, out they go to perform God's will with their will; and, zap, they are defeated. It is not enough to know what God's will is for our lives. We must wait for the Holy Ghost before we seek to do that will (Sometimes …, no many times, the wait is in years).

This was the major temptation Jesus was dealing with in the garden. Jesus knew what God the Father's will for his life was. No question about it, Jesus was to go to the cross and die for his people. Jesus declared this openly in Matthew 16, 17, 20, and John 12. Also, the entire Old Testament pointed to the cross. Yet, our Lord knew the will of God must be done through the power of God, and not out of commitment. Nowhere in the Bible are we called on to be committed. After all, this is what Peter had plenty of, and we see where it got him. We are called over and over again to obey, simply obey. For only through obedience will the Holy Ghost empower us to fulfill the will of God in our lives. Again, prayer is the key to not only knowing what God's will is, but in knowing when God wants his will to be done, and this takes time. However, prayer is urgent, "what, could you not watch with me one hour?" (Matthew 26:40).

I

The third aspect of the oil press experience deals with our desires, our feelings.

I know every Christian desires above all else to please God. Just as a child seeks to please their parents, so too do we seek to please our Father in heaven. However, just as a child falls short, so too do we, but it's not from lack of desire. So we try harder, but end up with the same sorry results until like Paul, we say:

> *For that which I do I allow not: for what I would, that do I not;*
> *but what I hate, that do I. For I know that in me (that is, in my*
> *flesh), dwelleth no good thing: for to will is present with me; but*
> *how to perform that which is good I find not. For the good that*
> *I would I do not: but the evil which I would not, that I do.*
> *Romans 7:15, 18, 19*

All those years Peter had walked with our Lord, and he still insisted:

> *Though I should die with thee, yet will I not deny thee.*
> *Matthew 26:35*

Despite Peter's determination, commitment and desire, he failed miserably, and he would have continued to do so until he experienced the oil press in his life. Just as Peter had to experience the oil press, so too must every Christian. That is, if we truly want to please God the Father. It is a must, yet it is at this very place, the garden experience, that so many, "stop their ears that they should not hear" (Zechariah 7:11). However, there are those that truly do identify, have surrendered their wills, and their every desire is to please the Lord, nevertheless, there still is no power from on high. What then? These are the ones, like Paul, cry out:

> *O wretched man that I am! Who shall deliver me from the body*
> *of this death.*
> *Romans 7:24*

Now we are ready for the oil press. Now, that we have become obedient, honest and empty, get ready for a visit from the very Spirit of Christ.

CHAPTER FOURTEEN

OBEDIENT, HONEST AND EMPTY

If Peter didn't experience the oil press in the Garden of Gethsemane, where did he? We serve a gracious and loving God. He knows we try so hard to please him; nevertheless, he will not intervene in our lives as long as we continue to strive from our own efforts. No, he waits until we are emptied of ourselves. That is what happened to Peter.

OBEDIENT

We next find Peter at Galilee. Apparently Peter left Jerusalem after the death, burial and resurrection of the Lord. This was the Lord's last instructions to the disciples just prior to their entering the Garden, "but after I am risen again, I will go before you into Galilee" (Matthew 26:32).

One thing about Peter, he may have been defeated, but he remained obedient. He obeyed the Lord, and in his defeat went to Galilee. He didn't find the Lord there as expected, so Peter did the only thing he knew to do. He went fishing.

> *There were together Simon Peter, and Thomas called Didymus,*
> *and Nathanael of Cana in Galilee, and the Sons of Zebedee, and*
> *two other of his disciples. Simon Peter saith unto them, I go*
> *afishing.*
>
> *John 21:2, 3*

This didn't mean he was going to fish to pass the time of day. No, Peter in affect said, I quit this discipleship stuff. I'm going back to being a fisherman as I was before I ever heard of Jesus. Being his disciple is finished; no more, gone, kaput. Six other disciples quit too.

> *They say unto him, we also go with thee. They went forth, and*
> *entered into a ship immediately.*
>
> *John 21:3*

So, the church was finished; or was it? You see, God is patient. He will wait. He will wait until we come to the end of ourselves. There is only one way God operates, and that is his way. He will wait. He will wait.

They fished all night and caught nothing. Not even one little fish was caught. God purposed it that way. Yes, there are times God actually wants us to fail. Not only had Peter come to his end emotionally, now he was exhausted physically as well. Now, the Lord could work a work in Peter's life. Now, Peter was ready to experience the oil press. Now that Peter was emptied of his determination, commitment and his desires, the Lord moved swiftly.

> *...When morning was now come, Jesus stood on the shore...*
> *John 21:4*

With you too; he will wait for you to come to your end. He might even see that you fail at your earthly endeavors. However, that is only to cause you to come to your end sooner.

We do notice one thing here. Despite Peter's failure and denial, Peter did obey. He went to Galilee as instructed. To obey is critical. Basically, that is all the Lord requires of us, to obey (Please know, going to Galilee wasn't out of commitment. Peter had no commitment left in him. This was strictly an act of obedience).

We know what happened next. Jesus showed up on the beach and called out to them to go ahead and cast the net one more time, but this time to the other side of the boat. Note: This wasn't a lack of skill on their part, because only six feet away, the width of the boat was a net full of fish (This is how I know the inability to catch anything earlier was planned by the Lord).

> *Then Jesus saith unto them, children, have ye any meat? They*
> *answered him, no. And he said unto them, cast the net on the*
> *right side of the ship, and ye shall find. They cast therefore, and*
> *now they were not able to draw it for the multitude of fishes.*
> *John 21:4-6*

Jesus had their attention.

HONEST

It wasn't long and Peter was again face to face with his Lord. Imagine, the last time Peter looked into those eyes, a cock was crowing for that third time. The one he had denied was again face to face with him.

This was not a time for joy. Peter had denied Jesus before Calvary, and now Peter had quit him here in Galilee. Peter must have been thinking what good am I to the Lord now. Just to the contrary, this is the time we are most good to him. This is where the Lord wants all of us to come to, the point of emptiness.

> *Jesus saith unto them, come and dine. And none of the disciples durst*
> *ask him, who art thou? Knowing that it was the Lord. Jesus then*
> *cometh, and taketh bread, and giveth them, and fish likewise. This is*
> *now the third time that Jesus shewed himself to the disciples, after*
> *that he was risen from the dead.*
> *John 21:12-14*

Peter is ready to experience what he had slept through earlier. Please look, the oil press isn't difficult. It doesn't require talent or abilities. No, the Lord's burden is light.

> *Come unto me all ye that labor and are heavy laden, and I will*
> *give you rest. Take my yoke upon you, and learn from me; for*
> *I am meek and lowly in heart: and ye shall find rest unto your*
> *soul. For my yoke is easy, and my burden is light.*
> *Matthew 11:28-30 (1)*

Jesus turns to Peter. This is the moment Peter had dreaded since his denial of the Lord.

So when they had dined, Jesus saith to Simon Peter, Simon,
son of Jonas, lovest thou me more than these?
John 21:15a

Oh no, the dreaded question, however, Peter replied only as he could.

He saith unto him, yea, Lord; thou knowest that I love thee.
John 21:15b

There is something unusual here in this exchange, but it cannot be picked up in the English translation. The Greek text, however, reveals the significance of what is being said here. There are four words for love in the Greek language: stergein, eran, philein and agapan. (2)

Stergein is a love that has its basis in one's own nature. It speaks of the constitutional efflux of natural affection...Stergein is used in the New Testament in its noun form, with the letter alpha prefixed which negates the word, that is, makes it mean the opposite to what it meant in itself. It occurs in Romans 1:31 and Second Timothy 3:3 and is translated in both instances by the words "without natural affection...". (3)

Eran is a love that has its basis in passion...and is where we get our word erotic. This word for love is not found in the New Testament. (4)

Philein is used forty-five times in the New Testament, and is an unimpassioned love, and friendly love, a brotherly love. It is based upon an inner community between the person loving and the person or object loved. That is, both have things in common with one another. This is where we get our word Philadelphia, city of brotherly love. (5)

Agapan is a love that has its basis in preciousness, a love called out of one's heart by an awakened sense of value in the object loved that causes one to prize it. Agapan is God's love. This is the love found in John 3:16. The love exhibited at Calvary. It is the love that says, I have decided to love you no matter what you do to me. You cannot cause me not to love you. This is unconditional love. (6)

In our English translation of the Bible we lose the richness of the Greek. Without the Greek we would miss the full significance of this exchange that is taking place between Peter and the Lord. However, we do have the Greek and we are able to share this with you.

When Jesus asked Peter, "lovest thou me?" The word our Lord used was agapas (form of agapan). He was saying to Peter, do you agapan love me, or do you love me unconditionally?

Peter's reply was, "yea Lord, thou knowest that I love thee". The word Peter used for love was philo (a form of philein). Peter was saying, yes I love you, but I can only love you as a brother. I cannot love you as you want me to love you.

At least Peter was being honest. Obedience and honesty; God can do something with those two attributes. Now watch what happens.

Again, Jesus asks Peter the same question.

He saith to him again the second time, Simon, son of Jonas, lovest
(agapas) thou me?
John 21:16

Again the Lord used agapas, and again Peter responded with philo.

He saith unto him, yea, Lord; thou knowest that I love (philo)
Thee.

John 21:16

Don't you know what was going through Peter's mind: Could it be what was racing through Peter's mind were the three times he denied Jesus a few days earlier. He had to be wondering how Jesus could ever forgive him after he had bragged so. However, Peter remained honest. He could not love Jesus as Jesus loved him. He couldn't, and now he was going to say so. One time before he told Jesus he could do it. He had said before that he would stand by him; even die with him. Peter now knows he can't do a thing on his own. He can't even agapan love the Son of God.

We can't either; not really. We can't do anything on our own. We too can't even love the Lord our God without him in us doing it through us.

Then in verse seventeen, Jesus asks a third time, and this time Peter was grieved. Without the Greek we would come away from this passage without a good understanding. What comes to our minds as to why Peter was grieved is Jesus had to ask him three times, corresponding to the three denials (Of course, this may have been partially so). However, the reason Peter was so grieved wasn't because Jesus asked three times. The reason for grieving was based on how Jesus asked the third time. The word love the Lord used this third time in verse seventeen wasn't agapas. It was phileis (form of philein).

He saith unto him the third time, Simon, son of Jonas, lovest (phileis)
thou me? Peter was grieved because he said unto him the third time,
lovest (phileis) thou me? And he said unto him, Lord, thou knowest
all things; thou knowest that I love (philo) thee.

John 21:17

In other words, Peter couldn't love the Son of God as Jesus wanted Peter to. That is OK, the Lord will come down to us, and accept whatever little love we can give him. In affect, Jesus is saying, Peter, I know you can't agapan love me, so give me what you can give, and I will use that.

EMPTY

The key was, although defeated, Peter was obedient. Then Peter was honest. Finally, Peter was emptied: emptied of his self, good self at that. Now the Lord could use Peter.

God doesn't need our abilities. He doesn't need our commitment, nor does God need our determination. All he wants is for us to be obedient, honest and empty. That is all: obey, be honest, and the empty will follow. That is what the oil press is all about. However, what lies at the center of the oil press experience is as much as it hurt Peter to admit his failings, Peter did not, "pull away the shoulder, and stop his ears, that he should not hear" (Zechariah 7:11).

Not only is the oil press experience necessary for a true Christian walk, but it is urgent.

...wherefore the rather, brethren, give diligence to make your calling
and election sure: for if ye do these things, ye shall never fall.
2Peter 1:10

Now, Peter was ready for the cross. Yes, the cross awaits all of us, but the garden must come first. Without the garden, the cross is of no avail. In fact, so many are struggling in their walk, and they attribute their trials as coming from the cross working in their lives. Yet, the fruits of the cross are absent. In fact, there is still so much anger, bitterness and strife present in their lives. Upon further examination, it is apparent these are still fighting the garden experience. They are so much like Peter, for they seek to walk with their own determination, desires and commitment. They are still very far removed from being obedient, honest and empty.

Be prepared, the garden experience may take years and years, because some of us are so committed, determined and able God has to chisel away at us over a long period before we actually become obedient, honest and empty. In the process, please don't, "…pull away the shoulder, and stop your ears, that you should not hear" (Zechariah 7:11).

---

(1) Isn't it interesting Jesus used the term soul? That is exactly what the oil press is all about: The surrender of our soul: our mind, will and feelings.

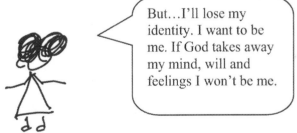

> But…I'll lose my identity. I want to be me. If God takes away my mind, will and feelings I won't be me.

What is there about you that is so precious that you want to keep it? Go on list what you like about yourself. Go on, and do it.

Now, which do you want more, God or your good qualities? You cannot have both, because these good things that you are holding on to are the very things standing between you and God.

You are going to have to make up your mind. Jesus said we must make up our mind. We cannot have it both ways.

> *If any one come to me, and hate not their father, and mother, and*
> *wife (husband), and children, and brethren, and sisters, yea and*
> *his own life (again the word for life here is the Greek word for*
> *soul) also, they cannot be my disciples.*
>
> *Luke 14:26*

Which do you want more; God or your goodness? The decision is yours. If you want your goodness, then go your way, for you have your reward. If you truly want God, then call out as did Job, for it is only the judgment of God that can cleanse us of our goodness. You will not regret it.

(2) Wuest's Word Studies Vol. III; by Kenneth S. Wuest; Wm. B. Eerdmans Publishing Co.; Grand Rapids, Michigan 49502; 1973; p.59, 109, 119.

(3) Ibid; p. 109

(4) Ibid; p. 110

(5) Ibid; p. 111

(6) Ibid; p. 115

CHAPTER FIFTEEN

THE MESSAGE, HE IS RISEN

Each of the three times Jesus asked Peter, "lovest thou me?" the Lord followed that question up with, "Feed my sheep". There is a binding relationship between our inward spiritual walk with the Lord and our outward evangelization to a lost world. When the one is sure and true the other will always be present. An inward life of prayer and the proclamation of the Gospel go hand in hand. However, prayer is the neglected step child of the church, whereas witnessing is the over indulged bully of the church. Thus, the church is crippled and misguided. Consequently, let us take a fresh look at what is involved in witnessing the Word of God.

If Jesus had come; performed miracles; taught as he did; prophesied as he did; then died; and that was that: Then Christians are a sad lot indeed.

> *If Christ has not been raised our preaching is useless and so is your faith.*
>
> *1 Corinthians 15:14*

The Christian faith rests on the resurrection of Jesus Christ; not on his good moral teachings. Even though he was the greatest teacher of all times; this isn't the essence of the Christian faith. The Christian faith does not rest on his prophecies; even though he was the greatest prophet of all times. The Christian faith is not based on the miracles Jesus performed. The essence of the Christian faith is the fact of the empty tomb.

If Jesus Christ is not raised from the dead his teachings are all lies. His prophecies are false; and his miracles are but cheap entertainment. Consequently, the question to be put forth to a lost world is on that Sunday morning was the tomb empty? After all, no one will argue the following:
1. We all know for sure Jesus of Nazareth lived.
2. We all know Jesus was a great man.
3. We all know this Jesus died on a cross.
4. We all know he was buried.

No one will argue these points. The only question is: Was the tomb empty? Lets' examine the facts, and believe it or not, Jesus' enemies provided the best proof for an empty tomb. By putting a guard and sealing the tomb, the chief priests actually proved the resurrection. They couldn't have been more stupid. Let me illustrate what I mean.

Yep, that's right.

Here we are at the grave-site. I am talking with the chief priests. No question, the tomb is empty, and you fellows say the disciples stole the dead body? "Yep, that's right". Let's get this straight. He died on the cross that Passover day at three O'clock. "Yep, that's right". Then this Joseph of Arimathea and Nicodemus laid him in this tomb. Then you went to Pilate, and he let you secure this grave with your own guard, and even put a seal on the grave. "Yep, that's right". Now you are telling me that there is no dead body in this tomb. "Yep, that's right". Why then would you want everybody to know the disciples stole the body? They came overpowered the guards; broke the seal; rolled the rock back; and ran off with the body leaving behind the linen in which he was wrapped in. That's a bit far fetched, isn't it?

In fifty days Peter will preach in the streets of Jerusalem, but all we will get from the chief priests is silence.

HE IS RISEN!
HE IS RISEN!

All the officials would have to do to shut Peter up was to go get the corpse out of that tomb (after all, they controlled the tomb), and parade that dead body up and down the streets of Jerusalem, and that would have been the end of Christianity. However, they never did that. Why not?

The officials didn't get the corpse out of the tomb, because the chief priests knew the tomb was empty. Their silence proves the tomb was empty, and they knew the disciples didn't steal the body, because the guards told them so. They, of all people knew the resurrection was true, and their silence proves it.

Why then were the chief priests so dumb as to place guards at the tomb? Because they could only think the way they could think. In fact, there is only one way any of us can think, and that is in terms of how we think. You can't think differently from how you think.

Girls can't think like boys. Boys can't think like girls. Sure, we can guess about the other, but the difference is there and will stay there. For the most part, men are "doers", and girls are "being" persons. Please understand, neither men nor women are wrong, but don't we always fight to change the other to our way of thinking? Sure we do, but it doesn't work, does it?

The emphasis I want to make is that a man can never know what it is to be a mother, and a woman can never know what it is to be a father. We can only think the way we think. Likewise, unsaved people cannot think like saved people. It is impossible for an unsaved person (who operates by the flesh) to understand a saved person (who operates by the spirit).

The man without the spirit does not accept the things that come
from the Spirit of God, for they are foolishness to him, and he
cannot understand them, because they are spiritually discerned.
1 Corinthians 2:14

Not only can the unsaved not think like the saved, the unsaved cannot up and decide to be saved. It is not their decision to make. How can they make a decision for the Lord if they are utterly unable to think like a saved person? It is impossible for an unsaved person to decide to be saved, impossible! Salvation is an act of God, not of man.

No, only the chosen are saved. Only they will respond to the call of the risen savior. Just as three thousand responded to the empty tomb and were saved, and the chief priests didn't. The chief priests knew for a fact the tomb was empty, yet they did not respond to Peter's preaching of the risen Christ. The three thousand didn't know the tomb was empty, but they did respond to Peter's preaching of the risen Lord. What made the difference? God made the difference: not knowledge, not insight, not understanding, but God and God alone ("…they were pricked in their heart…" Acts 2: 37). God had chosen the three thousand, and he had not chosen the chief priests despite the fact the chief priests knew Jesus had been raised from the dead.

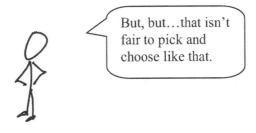

But, but…that isn't fair to pick and choose like that.

God doesn't have to save anyone. However, if you truly want to be saved, call upon him, and he will save you; because he said so:

Confess with your mouth that Jesus is Lord, and believe in your
heart that God raised him from the dead, you will be saved.
Romans 10:9

If you truly want to be saved he will surely save you.

What if he won't save me?

How badly do you want to be saved? If you want to be saved badly enough you will stay on your knees and call out to God until he saves you, and don't quit until he does. Show him how serious you are; or will you "pull away the shoulder, and stop your ears, that you should not hear", as did the chief priests? The choice is yours.

CHAPTER SIXTEEN

THE CONFLICT, MONEY

The following happened that resurrection morning as recorded in the Gospel of Matthew:

> *There was a violent earthquake; angel of the Lord came down; angel*
> *went to the tomb; rolled back the stone; sat on it; the guards were so*
> *afraid they shook; they became like dead men; angel spoke to the*
> *women; women hurried away; afraid yet filled with joy; ran to tell.*
>
> *Matthew 28:1-7*

Along with the women's reaction was the reaction of the guards:

> *...some of the watch came into the city, and shewed unto the chief*
> *priests all the things that were done.*
>
> *Matthew 28:11*

We assume the guard's story was the same story that the women told. Probably at the very same moment the one group (disciples) were being told, the other group (chief priests) were being told the identical story. It is safe to make this assumption, for it seems to be implied by Matthew.

You should have seen...there was a violent earthquake...angel of the Lord rolled back the stone...and the tomb was empty...there was no body...you've got to believe us.

Here we have two groups with two reactions at the same time to the same event: the disciples on one hand, and the chief priests on the other. Everyone agrees the tomb was empty. The issue is and always has been; why was the tomb empty.

The chief priests say the tomb was empty because the disciples stole the body (Remember, the guards didn't say this, only the priests said so). On the other hand, the disciples said the tomb was empty because Jesus Christ hath risen.

Chief Priests Reaction

1. Devised a plan.
2. Gave large sum of money.
3. Instructed guards to lie.
4. Will cover up the lie if they have to.
   They will lie about the lie.
5. Followed through with the plan.

Disciples Reaction

1. Afraid at first, and did not believe.
2. Later obeyed and went.
3. Worshipped the risen savior.

You can't get more opposite reactions to the same story at the very same time. I could perhaps understand two reactions that were a little different, but we have here two extremes. Why?

After all, you would think the chief priests would be happy Jesus was raised from the dead. You would think all Israel would welcome with open arms the news of an empty tomb. You would think all Jerusalem would have celebrated over a risen savior. But no, the world was angry about this Jesus of Nazareth being raised from the dead.

We cannot be sure why the chief priests and the elders of the people reacted so: Devised a plan; gave hush money; instituted a lie; developed a cover up (Matt. 28:12-14); then actively spread that lie. However, the Gospel of John gives us the most likely reason.

If we let him go on like this, everyone will believe in him, and then
the Romans will come and take away both our place and our nation.
John 11:48

It can be concluded the officials lied about what happened at the tomb that Sunday morning for the same reason they set into motion the scheme to kill Jesus.

1. "Everyone will believe." — Which translates: The people will leave and take their money with them.

2. "The Romans will come." — Without the money from the people the chief priests won't have any to give to Caesar, thus Caesar will send the troops.

3. "They will take away our place and nation." — The troops will dispose of the leaders. Other words, the chief priests will lose money, status, power, and their lives.

There is a similar problem here in America today between the church and the world. You would think the world would be happy someone was raised from the grave. Instead, the world is angry about this Jesus of Nazareth. Why?

I know: For the same reason the chief priests were angry. Everyone will believe, and the leaders will lose money, status and power. Jesus said this would happen.

...the world hates you.
John 15:19

Again, Jesus in his prayer to God the Father stated it this way:

I have given them thy word; and the world hath hated them,
because they are not of the world.
John 17:14

Paul puts it this way:

God forbid that I should glory, save in the cross of our Lord
Jesus Christ, by whom the world is crucified unto me, and I
unto the world.

Galatians 6:14

In other words, the world has nothing to offer a Christian (a truly born from above saint). Our identity is not found here. Our identity is found in Christ.

Peter tells us how to live in this world:

> *...as aliens and strangers in the world.*
> *1 Peter 2:11*

Yes, we have to live here, but we aren't to be controlled by this world or influenced by this world. Jesus said in the Sermon on the Mount that we must choose one or the other, but we can't have both; not even a little; it is all or none.

> *No one can serve two masters; either he will hate the one and love*
> *the other, or he will be devoted to the one and despise the other.*
> *You cannot serve both God and money.*
> *Matthew 6:24*

So, we are down to brass tacks. Money is the conflict. The world lives and dies on money. Money is the world's tool to motivate those of the world. Christians are to have the "mind of Christ", and our loyalties are for him. Christians, therefore, become a threat to the money men (the system). Christians then become dangerous people, because left to themselves, "...everyone will believe in him" (John 11:48). If everyone believes in this Jesus of Nazareth, the world then has no control over them, thus, "...the world hates you" (John 15:19).

CHAPTER SEVENTEEN

THE BATTLEFIELD, THE MIND

When we read, "...the world hates you" (John 15:19) could this be a bit too extreme? Sure, it is easy to see that the world doesn't like us, but hate...; that sounds too strong. If we won't believe what the Bible says concerning this matter, perhaps we might believe what the world has to say on this issue.

> Andrew Ure wrote in 1835, that it was nearly impossible to convert persons past the age of puberty, ...into useful factory hands. If young people could be prefitted to the industrial system, it would vastly ease the problems of industrial discipline later on. The result was...mass education.
> Built on the factory model, mass education taught basic reading, writing, and arithmetic, a bit of history and other subjects. This was the "overt curriculum." But beneath it lay an invisible or "covert curriculum" that was far more basic. It consisted and still does... of three courses: one in punctuality, one in obedience, and one in rote, repetitive work. Factory labor demanded workers who showed up on time,...It demanded workers who would take orders from management hierarchy without questioning. And it demanded men and women prepared to slave away at machines or in offices, performing brutally repetitious operations. (1)

Doesn't this bother you? The world openly admits that public education was installed to advance the establishment. They also admit that there was an overt curriculum and a covert curriculum in the schools and it is still there today.

I home school so all this doesn't concern me.

OK, if that doesn't bother you take a look at the following. Oh, I guess the following won't concern you either, because I'm sure you don't have a TV... You don't have a TV do you? Oh, I forget you only watch the good programs. Now that we have that settled, let us go a little further. This time we will look at the world of advertising, the very heart of the world system.

> Advertising is not what you do to a product. Advertising is what you do to the mind of the prospect. (2)

The basic approach of advertising is not to create something new

and different, but to manipulate what's already up there in the
mind, to retie the connections that already exist. (3)

These quotes come from the advertisers themselves, and they say these things so matter of fact. Are you bothered yet? Well, there is more:

The first thing you need to fix your message indelibly in the mind
is not a message at all. It is a mind: An innocent mind. A mind
that has not been burnished by someone else... (4)

Therefore, the world's target is to go after the children. The world's objective is to get children hooked on their product as soon as possible. After that, everything else is downhill. In other words, the one that gets to the children first will win the battle for the mind.
The world is serious, very serious in what they are doing. Listen to this statement.

Advertising is not a debate. It's a seduction. (5)

In case you might get the idea all this isn't as bad as I am portraying, look at this.

It is clear that advertising is entering a new era, an era that will
make the... (past decades)... look like a Sunday school picnic. (6)

The world is out to get you, or should I say, the world is out to get your mind which will result in getting your money. When an advertiser will spend 2.4 million dollars for a thirty second add in a Super Bowl, they know they will get back that money and much more. They know what they are doing, and they will spend even more next year, and the year after that, and the year after that, because they know you will buy more next year than you did this year, and the next year, and the next year after that: all because of that idol sitting in your living room (Or, I should say more accurately, the forty-two inch wall mounted high density surround sound idol in your entertainment center). Yes, we are in conflict with the world and its ways (or should be). The Lord knew about this some two thousand years ago.

No one can serve two masters. Either he will hate the one and love
the other, or he will be devoted to the one and despise the other.
You cannot serve both God and money.
Matthew 6:24

Paul said it this way.

I beseech ye therefore, brethren, by the mercies of God, that ye
present your bodies a living sacrifice, holy, acceptable unto
God, which is your reasonable service and be not conformed to
this world: but be ye transformed by the renewing of your
mind...
Romans 12:1, 2

In other words:

Set your minds on things above, not on earthly things.
Colossians 3:2

However, there is no way we can set our minds on things above as long as that TV maintains its prominent place in our homes (That doesn't even touch on the TV in our automobiles and the internet in our homes). How can we set our minds on the spiritual realm, when we are so surrounded and embedded in the fleshly realm? Yes, we are at war whether we like it or not, and the battlefield is the mind.

---

1. The Third Wave. Alvin Toffler, Bantam Book/published in association with William Morrow & Co., Inc. 1981. p. 29.
2. Positioning: The Battle for Your Mind. Al Ries and Jack Trout. Warner Books/published by arrangement with McGraw-Hill Book Company, 1221 Avenue of the Americas, New York, N.Y. 10020. 1986. p.2.
3. Ibid. p.5
4. Ibid. p.20
5. Ibid. p.60
6. Marketing Warfare. Al Ries and Jack Trout. A Plume Book, New American Library/ published by arrangement with McGraw Hill, Inc., 1221 Avenue of the Americas, New York, N.Y. 10020. 1986. p.40.
7. Opsit. p.6.

CHAPTER EIGHTEEN

THE STRATEGY, DEFENSE

A first reaction to this conflict with the world might be to go out and go toe to toe with the world system: to beat them at their own game. After all, the church has a much superior product. However, let me show you what happens when we do this.

In 1985 the per capita consumption of advertising in America was $376.62 (Yes, this is an old figure, but you will get the idea). If the church spent $1 million in advertising the true Gospel message we would be bombarding the consumer with less than ½ cent in advertising. The church would simply be changing things from $376.62 per year to $376.62 ½ per year of advertising consumed by the viewer. As you can see that would be a drop in the bucket, literally.

To do any good the church would have to spend hundreds of millions, even billions, on advertising the true Gospel to have any impact at all.

Going head to head with the world is not wise. First of all, we don't have that kind of money in the churches. Even if we did, this is not the way we are to go about proclaiming the Gospel. Most of all, however, the church was not called to witness in this fashion. Our Lord gives us the strategy we are to use. That strategy is laid out for us in Matthew chapter 28.

Once the tomb was found empty what was the next thing both sides did?

Church's Instructions	World's Instructions
1. "The angel said to the woman, come and see the place where he lay. Then go quickly and tell his disciples: He has risen from the dead."	1. "When the chief priests had met…and devised a plan, they gave the soldiers a large sum of money, telling them, you are to say, his disciples came during the night and stole him away while we were asleep… so the soldiers took the money and did as they were instructed."
2. "As they ran to tell…Suddenly Jesus met them…They worshipped him…Then Jesus said…Go and tell my brothers…"	2. "And this story has been widely circulated among the Jews to this very day."

The war was on! And we have been locked into mortal combat ever since. Right from the start, both sides used the same methods, word of mouth. However, the message and strategies are different.

[Note: Neither side disputes the fact of the empty tomb
…….the dispute is only over why the tomb was empty]

Most of all, we need to pay particular attention to the two distinctively different strategies.

Church's Strategy

1. Start at the bottom. Instead of saying, go tell Herod, Pilate or higher ups, and get to them before the guards do. No, go to our own first, and work out from there: fishermen, poor, the blind, lame, etc.

2. It is to be a grass-roots campaign: "go into all the world and preach the good news to all creation". Don't pick and choose. Tell whomever you come into contact with. Don't leave anyone out, especially the poor: "all creation", means earthy.

3. It is to be one on one…personal contact…eye to eye. "Go into all the world and preach the good news to all creation. Whoever believes… and is baptized will be saved, but whoever does not believe will be condemned" (MK 16: 15, 16). Note: "whoever equals everyone; these denote singular, not plural.

4. The motivation for this campaign is the Holy Spirit. "I am going to send you what my Father has promised; but stay in the city until you have been clothed with power from on high" (LK24:49).

World's Strategy

1. Start at the top. Start with the chief priests elders, the political leaders, those with influence, and those in leadership.

2. Go where the money is: "…this story has been widely circulated among the Jews". This equals the establishment: those in control; those in power.

3. Use mass strategy: "…this story has been widely circulated". "Widely" denotes a mass media concept.

4. The motivation for the world's campaign is money. "When the chief priests had met with the elders and devised a plan, they gave the soldiers a large (means lots and lots) sum of money…telling them, you are to say "So the soldiers took the money and did as they were instructed" (This was the first ad agency).

Let me sum up the two strategies:

Church
1. Start at the bottom
2. Grassroots centered
3. Personal contact
4. Holy Spirit is the motivation behind the church's campaign.

World
1. Start at the top
2. Establishment centered
3. Mass communication
4. Money is the motivation behind the world's campaign.

There is one last strategy difference:

5. The church is to wage a defensive war. Sorry to tell you this, but it is clear in the Bible that we are to maintain a defensive position during the war.

5. The world will wage an offensive war. They will come at us head on. They seek to hit us at our right and left flanks, even resort to gorilla warfare.

Satan, the world's commanding officer, would like nothing better than to get us to switch from a defensive strategy to an offensive strategy.

If you are a pastor, please relax, take a few deep breaths, and count to fifty slowly, then read on. You'll be fine, but please don't, "...pull away the shoulder, and stop your ears that you should not hear" (Zechariah 7:11). I know you have been brought up on offensive strategy. I too was taught the same thing; however, it never sat well with me. Now I know why: It is not scriptural. As the bride of Christ, the church is to assume a defensive position. We are not to take the offensive (Please understand, there is a difference between taking the initiative verses fighting an offensive battle. Also, we must remember the battlefield is not a geographical location. The battlefield is in the minds and hearts of the people, not a certain part of the country, nor the inner-city, etc.).

Now that we have paused, and taken several slow breaths, let us continue. Please bear with me on this, because it will change the way you read the Word of God, and in turn change the way you witness.

In discussing defensive warfare, I am going to the world first, not to the Bible. I shouldn't have to do this, because the Lord has already set forth how we are to do battle, and that should be that. However, I have seen over the years that so many church people believe the world before they will believe the Word. It's true, sad, but true. Bear with me on this please.

The first and most basic of war is all things being equal, the army with the most soldiers wins. (1)

Let me illustrate:

Church (offensive)	World (offensive)
[One hit out of every 3 shots]	
1st volley 60 soldiers x 1of 3= 20 hits	90 soldiers x 1of 3= 30 hits
2nd volley 30 soldiers x 1of 3= 10 hits	70 soldiers x 1of 3= 23 hits
3rd volley 7 soldiers x 1of 3= 2 hits	60 soldiers x 1of 3= 20 hits

War is over
in favor of larger army

The movies/TV portrays a handful of inspired men defeat hordes/hordes of Indians, but the bullets aren't real in the movies. When the bullets are for real, superior numbers win. Every general knows this. Why do you think we won WWII? Was it because we had superior trained troops? Sure, that accounted for some success, but the Germans and Japanese, both had brave well trained soldiers too. We won WWII because where the Germans or Japanese had two soldiers, we had four to six. Where the Germans or Japanese had four soldiers we had eight to ten. We won WWII, because we pounded them into submission. (2)

Yes, the smaller army can win, but it is not likely. We think of Gen. George Patton. He was a brilliant general. He was cunning. He had the best trained army ever. However, his brilliance, cunning and well trained army were not the secret to his success. Patton did so well because he had the Germans vastly outnumbered. Patton wasn't stupid. He knew where victory was. All these other things simply made the victory come quicker, and made victory more sure. (3)

"The free world applauded when Patton raced across France, but the truth is, we would have won without him." (4)

We saw before: "In the open field a fire fight between two squads is rapidly decided in favor of the larger unit. However, things change when one side goes defensive. (5)

Church (defensive)	World (offensive)
[1 hit out of every 3]	[1 hit out of every 9]
1st volley 60 soldiers x 1of 3= 20 hits	90 soldiers x 1of 9= 10 hits
2nd volley 50 soldiers x 1of 3= 17 hits	70 soldiers x 1of 9= 8 hits
3rd volley 42 soldiers x 1of 3= 14 hits	53 soldiers x 1of 9= 6 hits
4th volley 36 soldiers x 1of 3= 12 hits	39 soldiers x 1of 9= 4 hits
5th volley 32 soldiers x 1of 3= 10 hits	27 soldiers x 1of 9= 3 hits

War soon to be over
in favor of the smaller defensive army

Are we beginning to see why football coaches say, "offense gets the glamour, but defense wins football games". (6)

"In the Korean war, America won in the south on defense and lost in the north on offense." (7)

"England lost in the colonies on offense and won at Waterloo on defense." (8)

The reason I went into such detail here was to help show you that it isn't negative to take the defensive. In fact, to fight a defensive war makes sense from a worldly point of view, but even more importantly, we are called by the Lord to fight a defensive war anyway.

Ephesians 6:10-17, tells us three times to, "stand": verse eleven, "stand against the wiles of the devil"; verse thirteen, "stand your ground"; verse fourteen, "stand firm".

You can't get more defensive than that. We are clearly called into a defensive strategy. It can't be said more clearly.

Now look at the devil's strategy here in Ephesians. His weapon against us is clearly offensive: "flaming arrows" (Eph. 6:16).

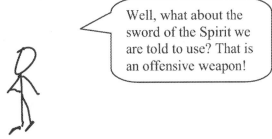

Well, what about the sword of the Spirit we are told to use? That is an offensive weapon!

Sorry, but the sword Paul describes here in Ephesians is the Roman soldiers short sword, and the Romans used that sword for defense. If the Roman soldier used the short sword for offense he would be off balance, thus exposing himself to the enemy. I know we have been told the sword here in Ephesians is an offensive weapon, but those that told us this are misinformed. All the weapons listed here in Ephesians by Paul are strictly defensive. The weapon the Roman soldier used for offense was the spear or lance, not the short sword. Isn't it interesting the weapon the Roman soldier used against the Lord that day on the cross was the spear, the offensive weapon.

We must see that the devil is fighting an offensive battle against us, and we must keep him in that posture. Earlier in Ephesians Paul tells us this:

...neither give place to the devil
Ephesians 4:27

"Place", denotes defensive. The NIV says it this way: "…do not give the devil a foothold". That is clearly a defensive position. James says it this way: "…Resist the devil, and he will flee from you" (James 4:7). Again, we are to assume a defensive position. In this way it keeps the devil on the offensive, which, as we know, is the least desirable strategy. Peter also tells us to maintain the defense.

> *Be self controlled and alert. Your enemy the devil prowls around*
> *like a roaring lion looking for someone to devour. Resist him,*
> *standing firm in the faith…*
> *1 Peter 5:8, 9*

Without question, these verses present both strategies, that of the church and that of the enemy. Once again we are told to maintain a defensive position: Whereas, the devil is clearly on the offense. That is great. Let's keep it that way.

OK, what is meant by defense? In war here in the physical world, defense is geographical location and structure. We, however, are dealing with the spiritual realm.

First, let me tell you what I don't mean:

I don't mean for us to dig foxholes all around our homes and the church building.

I don't mean for us to buy firearms and all the ammunition we can get hold of.

I don't mean for us to stash a two year supply of food in the church building.

No, countries and cities are not the battlefield. The battlefield we are engaged in has no geographical location. The minds and hearts of the people is the battlefield. Therefore, to fight a defensive war in the minds and hearts of the people, we are to stand on what already is.

> *Then Jesus came to them and said, all authority in heaven and on*
> *earth has been given to me.*
> *Matthew 28:18*

What were his next words? Look closely.

> *Go ye therefore,…*
> *Matthew 28:19*

Consequently, the basis for our going is what?

"…has been given", is the basis for our going, and we can easily see that, "has been given", is already done. Therefore, our going is based on something that has already been done, and won't ever be undone. Our going in this time and place is based on a past completed action done by Jesus Christ. So, our message is to be: THE TOMB IS EMPTY, AND THE REASON THE TOMB IS EMPTY IS BECAUSE HE IS RISEN!

We are defending facts; the facts of a risen savior.

Look at Peter's first sermon. All Peter does is state one fact after another in Acts 2.

Fact#1. What you see is what Joel spoke of in Joel 2:28-32 (Acts2:14-21).

Fact#2. Jesus lived, died and was buried (Acts2:22, 23).

Fact#3. There was an empty tomb (Acts2:24a).

Fact#4. Reason for the empty tomb was that God raised Jesus from the dead. (Acts2:24).

Fact#5. This is fulfillment of Psalm 16:8-11 (Acts2:25-28).

Fact#6. Go look for yourselves at the empty tomb (Acts2:29-32).

Fact#7. Not only was this Jesus of Nazareth raised from the dead, but he is right now at the right hand of God (Acts2:33, 34).

Fact#8. Peter then declared, "This Jesus, whom you crucified is both Lord and Christ" (Acts2:36).

Peter was completely defensive. He stood on what already was and is. He never sought to debate with the people. He did not seek to convince people of the benefits of being a Christian, and he did not seek to get them to understand the situation. He simply stated the facts of the matter.

You see, once we enter into a debate with the lost (unbelievers), we concede our defensive position, and go on the offensive, and the devil likes us to do this, because now we are using our defensive weapons on the offense, and at that point we become vulnerable to the devil's fiery darts. We are off balance.

Let me say this another way: If we seek to change the minds of the lost, and try to convince them to become Christian; that means we admit that they belong to Satan, and we are to wrestle them away from the devil.

Nobody belongs to Satan. Everyone belongs to God. Even if someone dies and goes to hell they don't belong to Satan. Satan has no rights. Satan has no authority over anyone, because all authority (not most, but all), has been given to Jesus Christ. Satan does not send people to hell, God does. However, time after time Christians seek to "woo" the lost to the Lord. This kind of strategy is offensive strategy, because we are seeking to convince them to come over to our side. If that be the case, it must mean Satan has the victory with the individual, and we seek to secure the victory all over again for Jesus. Church, we have the victory already.

> *Having disarmed the powers and authorities, he made a public*
> *spectacle of them, triumphing over them by the cross.*
> *Colossians 2:15*

The verbs in this verse are all past tense. When we talk offensive strategy we are actually crucifying Jesus all over again. We, in affect, are saying what Jesus did on the cross wasn't good enough.

When witnessing, instead of trying to get people to change their minds about the way they are living, simply declare the Lordship of Christ as it is. Proclaim the Gospel one fact after another. In other words, be a witness. After all, this is what the Lord said to be:

> *...you'll be my witnesses.*
> *Acts 1:8*

1. <u>Marketing Warfare,</u> Al Ries and Jack Trout. A Plume Book, New American Library, 1633 Broadway, New York, New York 10019. Copyright 1986. p.1.
2. Ibid.
3. Ibid.
4. Ibid. p. 193
5. Ibid. p. 31
6. Ibid. p. 33
7. Ibid. p. 33
8. Ibid. p. 33

Following are more quotes from the world's perspective concerning the battle for the mind, and are found in:

<u>Positioning: The Battle for Your Mind.</u> Al Ries and Jack Trout. Warner Books/published by arrangement with McGraw-Hill Book Company, 1221 Avenue of the Americans, New York, N.Y. 10020. 1986.

"Millions of dollars have been wasted trying to change minds with advertising. Once a mind is made up, it's almost impossible to change." p.6

"Our extravagant use of communications to solve a host of business and social problems has so jammed our channels that only a tiny fraction of all messages actually gets through. And not necessarily the most important ones either." p.11

"The mind rejects new information that doesn't compute. It accepts only that new information which matches its current state of mind. It filters out everything else." p.29

"Not only does the human mind reject information which does not match its prior knowledge or experience, it doesn't have much prior knowledge or experience to work with." p.30

CHAPTER NINETEEN

BUT SOME DOUBTED

There are three reactions to the fact of the empty tomb, and all of us fall into one of these three categories.

The first reaction to the fact of the empty tomb is worship.

> *...and they came and held him by the feet, and worshipped him.*
> *Matthew 28:9*

The second reaction to the fact of the empty tomb is resentment, retaliation, and hostility.

> *And when they were assembled with the elders, and had taken*
> *counsel, they gave large sum of money unto the soldiers, saying,*
> *say ye, his disciples came by night, and stole him away while we*
> *slept. And if this come to the governor's ears, we will persuade*
> *him, and secure you.*
> *Matthew 28:12-14*

Later these same officials will retaliate against the church. Finally, they will unleash extraordinary hostility towards the bride of Christ, the church.

Both of these first two reactions have several things in common. In each of these reactions, both acknowledge the tomb was empty. This is an important fact, and we need to put our finger on this.

The authorities' reaction to the empty tomb wasn't disbelief. They never questioned the guards as to the validity of the existence of the empty tomb. Instead, the authorities immediately set about to cover up the fact of why the tomb was empty. In fact, the cover up confirmed the truthfulness of the empty tomb. They simply resented, retaliated against, and became hostile towards that empty tomb and the risen Savior. Therefore, both those that worshipped the Lord, and those that became hostile believed the tomb was empty.

The second similarity of these two reactions was the fact both groups acted in an overt and outward manner. Consequently, these two reactions have more in common to each other than does the third reaction have with either of these two.

The third reaction to the empty tomb is doubt. As we will see, doubt is the most devastating reaction to the fact of the empty tomb.

> *...and when they saw him, they worshipped him: but some*
> *doubted.*
> *Matthew 28:17*

This third reaction to the empty tomb is separate and different from the other two. In this reaction, those that doubted questioned the empty tomb and a risen Savior; and this unbelief was covert and hidden. Their doubt was shrouded in the cloak of false worship. Therefore, it is easier for a person to change from the second reaction to the first than it is to change from the third reaction to the first. It is easier to go from hostility to true worship than it is to go from false worship to true worship. Most importantly, however, is that the greatest damage to the Christian faith comes from within the worshipers rather than from the hostile elements without the church. (1)

These facts are clearly seen in the months and years after the resurrection where many of these very same openly hostile priests became true worshipers of the risen Lord.

> *And the word of God increased; and the number of disciples*
> *multiplied in Jerusalem greatly; and a great company of the*
> *priests were obedient to the faith.*
>
> *Acts 6:7*

We also have the Apostle Paul's testimony to these facts. He, of all people, was the most hostile towards the risen Jesus Christ, yet, later he too truly worshipped the Lord, even unto the giving of his life.

It isn't impossible for a doubter to eventually come to be a true worshiper, but it is more difficult, because there are some serious pitfalls inherent in doubting that you don't find in open resentment.

Doubting is a serious malady. If doubt persists in a worshiper's life it will turn into hatred, contempt, and calumny.

Who do you suppose Zechariah was dealing with (Please see chapter three)? Sure, it was false worshipers, doubters.

The whole while Zechariah was in Jerusalem rebuilding, he dealt with those that resented him, and who were openly hostile towards him, but these people didn't give Zechariah nearly the problems the false worshipers gave him. In fact, it was the new comers, the doubters, that killed Zechariah; not those that were openly hostile towards him for all those many years. In the end the false worshipers, those from within the church, that took Zechariah and killed him, "…between the temple and the alter" (Matthew 23:35).

Yes, if doubting persists it will turn to hatred, contempt, and calumny; and it all starts with the "…pulling away of the shoulder". Then it moves to, "…the stopping of the ears, that they should not hear, …". And finally, "…the heart becomes as an adamant stone" (Zechariah 7:11).

Yes, doubters are church people. They look like Christians, act like Christians, talk like Christians, but inside they still don't believe the empty tomb. They may say they believe, but their actions betray them (Please see Vol. III).

Please understand, I am not saying these doubters are evil people with evil intent. Quite to the contrary, these doubters, for the most part, are good people; living good lives, and do good things for others. You might say they do the right thing, at the right time, in the right place.

These doubters have the best intentions. They even attend church regularly. Often the doubters are the very leaders of the church. In reality they are causing the most damage to the bride of Christ, the church itself. (2)

Hey, what about John the Baptist?

Yeah, he doubted when he asked Jesus, "Art thou he that should come, or do we look for another?"

Let's take a look at that in the following chapter.

---

1. Notice: Never does anyone go from belief to unbelief. It is impossible to have a true experience with the risen Lord, and later doubt this Jesus. If someone does appear to do this, then belief was a put on, a mask. If someone is sure of a risen savior, they are always sure. This is why true believers will, and do, die for their faith.

2. Dietrich Bonhoeffer refers to these false worshipers as those that operate from human love instead of spiritual love (Jesus Christ is the center of the worship of those that exhibit spiritual .love, and the center of human love are other persons).   Acceptance is the motivation of false worshipers, whereas Christ is the motivation for true worshipers. You might say, what's wrong with loving others? There isn't anything wrong with loving others. The problem is that those that love from human love aren't honest about their worship. They aren't truly worshiping Jesus Christ. Their focus is on people, not Christ. These in many cases don't recognize what they are doing (Only through experiencing the oil press in one's life do we come to know the difference).

> Often it (human love) far surpasses genuine Christian love in fervent devotion and visible results. It speaks the Christian language with overwhelming and stirring eloquence. But it is what Paul is speaking of when he says: "And though I bestow all my goods to feed the poor, and though I give my body to be burned"- In other words, though I combine the utmost deeds of love with the utmost devotion- "and have not charity (that is, the love of Christ), it profiteth me nothing" (ICor.13:3). Human love is directed to the other person for his own sake, spiritual love loves him for Christ's sake. Therefore, human love seeks direct contact with the other person; it loves him not as a free person but as one whom it binds to itself. It wants to gain, to capture by every means; it uses force… Human love has little regard for truth. It makes the truth relative,...human love is by its very nature desire…so long as it can satisfy this desire in some way, it will not give it up, even for the sake of truth,…But where it can no longer expect its desire to be fulfilled, there it stops short…There it turns into hatred, contempt, and calumny. (Life Together, by Dietrich Bonhoeffer; Harper, San Francisco: A Division of Harper Collins Publishers; 1954. p.33-34).

CHAPTER TWENTY

OF THE SAME MIND

Just prior to John the Baptist's death at the hands of King Herod, he sent a message to Jesus.

> *Now when John had heard in the prison the works of Christ, he*
> *sent two of his disciples, and said unto him, Art thou he that*
> *should come, or do we look for another?*
>> *Matthew 11:2, 3*

If that is a question of doubt, then much of the Bible is a lie. If that was a question of doubt, then Jesus cannot be the Christ.

I repeat doubt is the major enemy to the church.

It was doubt that kept the nation Israel out of the Promised Land. It was belief that made it possible for Joshua and Caleb to enter into the Promised Land (Numbers 13:26-34, 38). In fact, disbelief (doubt) was the reason the Old Nation Israel was "cut off", and in its place the church was established (Not to replace the Old Nation Israel, but to be God's continued witness in the world, as well as being laborers in the harvest).

> *...because of unbelief they were broken off, and thou (the church)*
> *standest by faith.*
>> *Romans 11:20*

Once the church lives by doubt (unbelief) then God will cut it off just as assuredly as he cut off the Old Nation Israel for their doubt.

> *For if God spared not the natural branches, take heed lest he*
> *also spare not thee.*
>> *Romans 11:21*

This right here is the essence of the Bible: both in the Old Testament and the New Testament. All of scripture rests on this fact. How then, can Jesus commend John the Baptist for doubting when unbelief is the major sin?

> *Verily I say unto you, among them that are born of women there*
> *hath not risen a greater than John the Baptist...*
>> *Matthew 11:11*

If Jesus was in fact praising John for doubting; he, in essence, was doing the work of Satan. Also, you can't have salt water and fresh water come from the same well. It must be one or the other, but not both (James 3:11-12). A tree either produces good fruit or bad fruit, but not both (Matthew 12:33). Jesus is either Lord, or he isn't. He cannot be both. He cannot chastise some for doubting, and here praise John the Baptist for his doubts.

...he appeared unto the eleven..., and upbraided them with
their unbelief...
Mark 16:14

If Jesus had answered John the Baptist with a simple yes or no that would have been one thing, but Jesus in answering John, gave him the highest praises of all:

Verily I say unto you, among them that are born of woman there
hath not risen a greater than John the Baptist...
Matthew 11:11

These two cannot exist together: doubt and honor.

We must see this. We are merrily going our way as if nothing is wrong, and we giddily justify ourselves by this very passage of scripture right here.

I realize almost every pastor on this planet has preached this passage was a question of doubt. Books have been written in this same vain: justifying doubt, and implying it has some virtue. Also, by treating John the Baptist's question as a question of doubt, we are deluding ourselves into a state of complacency, just as did Peter when he fell asleep in the Garden of Gethsemane.

Worse yet, by treating the Baptist's question as doubt, we are making doubt to be good, thus sin is good. In fact, doubt becomes a desirable quality.

Verily I say unto you, among them that are born of women there
hath not risen a greater than John the Baptist: not withstanding
he that is least in the kingdom of heaven is greater than he.
Matthew 11:11

John doubts and is praised. We doubt and are praised even more. However, it goes even further still. We teach doubt from one generation to another. As if that isn't enough, we actually become angry towards those that disagree with our doubt.

We have made up to be down, and down to be up, and don't let anyone get in our way. We have actually become the worst enemy to our head, Jesus Christ.

We must remember. We are not dealing with a bumbling idiot with a long tail, horns and a pitchfork. Satan is a genius, and we are acting like Peter: We seek to overcome by determination, commitment and ability. We simply fall right into the devil's hands; and love every minute of it as we go merrily on our way. Wake up, wake up; we are sleeping through the Garden of Gethsemane experience as did the three disciples.

Yawn...man...I sure don't see it...yawn...that way.

Please turn the TV off as I show you beyond a doubt that this question by John the Baptist was not a question of doubt.

> *Now when John had heard in the prison the works of Christ, he sent*
> *two of his disciples, and said unto him, Art thou he that should*
> *come, or do we look for another?*
> *Jesus answered and said unto them, Go and shew John again those*
> *things which ye do hear and see: The blind receive their sight, and*
> *the deaf hear, and dead are raised up, and the poor have the gospel*
> *preached to them.*
> *And blessed is he, whosoever shall not be offended in me.*
> *And as they departed, Jesus began to say unto the multitudes concerning*
> *John, What went ye out into the wilderness to see? A reed shaken with*
> *the wind? But what went ye out for to see? A man clothed in soft*
> *raiment? Behold, they that wear soft clothing are in kings' houses.*
> *But what went ye out for to see? A prophet? Yea, I say unto you, and*
> *more than a prophet. For this is he, of whom it is written, Behold, I*
> *send my messenger before thy face, which shall prepare thy way before*
> *thee. Verily I say unto you, Among them that are born of women*
> *there hath not risen a greater than John the Baptist: notwithstanding*
> *he that is least in the kingdom of heaven is greater than he.*
> *Matthew 11:2-11*

The first clue this is not a question of doubt comes from Jesus himself. After John's disciples departed to go back to John in prison, Jesus asked some questions of the multitude.

> *What went ye out into the wilderness to see? A reed shaken with*
> *the wind? But what went ye out for to see? A man clothed in soft*
> *raiment?...But what went ye out for to see? A prophet?*
> *Matthew 11:7-9*

We can easily see the answer to each question here in verses seven to nine was found within the questions themselves. Even the least of the multitude could see this (No, no, I should say, especially the least of the multitude could see this). Likewise, the least of the multitude could see the same thing in John's question about Jesus. The answer to John's question was found in the question itself.

Anybody (and everybody) that knew John, in even the slightest, knew without a doubt John was not, "a reed shaken with the wind". In fact, he was the very opposite, and the least of the least knew this most of all (The multitude may not have been able to read nor write, but they in many respects were much wiser than those in king's palaces).

If you had eyes at all you knew John the Baptist never wore "soft raiment". In fact, it was common knowledge John had one outfit, and only one outfit.

> *And the same John had his raiment of camel's hair, and a leather*
> *girdle about his loins; and his meat was locusts and wild honey.*
> *Matthew 3:4*

Even the blind knew this (No, especially the blind knew this). Likewise, everyone knew John the Baptist could never be found in "king's houses". There was one place, and one place only to find John the Baptist: "in the wilderness". Even the lame knew this (No, especially the lame knew this). If you wanted to find John you had to go where he was. He never lived in a house or in the city. Ask any lame person and they would tell you this with absolute assurance. They never had a doubt.

After listening to John for but a moment there was but one conclusion that could be drawn from his words: John the Baptist, of all people, was without a doubt a prophet. Even the deaf knew this (No, especially the deaf knew this). Listen, even King Herod, the man that imprisoned and killed John, knew that John was a prophet.

> *For Herod feared John, knowing that he was a just man and an*
> *holy, and observed (kept him safe) him; and when he heard him,*
> *he did many things, and heard him gladly.*
>
> *Mark 6:20*

Consequently, the blind, lame and deaf knew the answers to Jesus' questions concerning John the Baptist. In fact, the questions weren't questions at all. They were answers to questions that never needed to be asked (That is, if you were part of the multitude).

Anyone that knew Jesus would know the answer to John's question before it was asked. In fact, the question never needed to be asked. The fact it was asked meant to the multitude it was the very answer to itself. The blind, lame and deaf knew this. No, I must say again it was the blind, lame and deaf that knew most of all the question was the answer to itself.

> *...go and shew John again those things which ye do hear and see:*
> *the blind receive their sight, and the lame walk, the leapers are*
> *cleansed, and the deaf hear,...*
>
> *Matthew 11:4-5*

Oh, poor Christian, what is wrong when we doubt so. Perhaps, it would be better we were blind. Then we would have an excuse for our doubt. If the blind can see what we cannot see, then may we become blind?

> *And Jesus said, for judgment I am come into this world, that they*
> *which see not might see; and that they which see might be made*
> *blind.*
>
> *John 9:39*

Dear Christian, we see yet we are so blind. We have legs yet we know not where we go; and we have ears to hear, yet we understand not: all because we are sleeping through the oil press. We seek to "do" for him rather than "be" who we are to be.

Not only are we trying to do before we are, but when we do, we see up as down, and down as up. We see an answer as a question. Yet, we can find no answers to our questions. We see doubt as faith, and doubt our faith.

The second and third clues to the fact that this was not a question of doubt can be found in comparing Scripture with Scripture.

But let him ask in faith, nothing wavering...for let not that man
think that he shall receive anything of the Lord.

James 1:6, 7

If John's question was a question of doubt, then according to James, John should not have received even so much as a reply from the Lord. To the contrary, Jesus gave John the highest complement ever given. Either James doesn't know what he is talking about or Jesus doesn't. That is, if this is a question of doubt. If James is correct then that makes Jesus to be, "a wave of the sea driven with the wind and tossed" (James 1:6). After all, Jesus rebukes others of little faith, but won't rebuke John. That makes Jesus wishy-washy at best. Jesus cannot be wishy-washy and be "King of Kings" at the same time. Consequently, this could not, and was not, a question of doubt.

Next, in the Gospel of Luke, while John the Baptist was still in his mother's womb, he recognized Jesus, who, likewise was in Mary's womb.

And it came to pass, that, when Elizabeth heard the salutation
of Mary, the babe (John the Baptist) leaped in her womb; and
Elizabeth was filled with the Holy Ghost.

Luke 1:41

How is it, John in his mother's womb before taking his first breath could recognize the baby Jesus, yet here thirty years later in prison John doubts Jesus is the Christ? One or the other is not true. Which one is it? Is Luke wrong, or could it be John isn't asking a question of doubt?

Then again, how could John the Baptist be so sure Jesus was who he was at the baptism of Jesus, however, ten months later in prison John is not so sure?

The next day John seeth Jesus coming unto him, and saith, Behold
the lamb of God, which taketh away the sin of the world. This is
he of whom I said, After me cometh a man which is preferred
before me; for he was before me.

John 1:29-30

No matter which one you pick; the baptism or in prison, it makes John to be exactly what Jesus said he wasn't "a reed shaken with the wind" (Matthew 11:7).

Not only was John sure at the baptism, he declared that he, "...bare record" (John 1:32); and in John 1:34 he repeated that with: "...I say, and bear record that this is indeed the Son of God".

And John bare record, saying, I saw the Spirit descending from
heaven like a dove, and it abode upon him...And I saw, and bare
record that this is the Son of God.

John 32, 34

By using this legal language, John couldn't have been more precise and sure that Jesus was he to whom we were looking for. How can we then preach that John doubted only ten months later in prison?

Come now pastors, tell me which scriptures are true and which aren't. Did Mary and Elizabeth tell Luke the truth? Did they make up the story of the baby leaping in the womb? Was John sure at Jesus' baptism, but not so sure in prison? If he was sure at the baptism, but doubted when he was in prison then by definition he wasn't sure at the baptism.

If John wasn't sure at the baptism then what kind of prophet is it that doesn't recognize the fulfillment of his own prophecy? After all, that is the definition of a prophet: He knows what he is talking about for he speaks for God. Which is it, or is John the Baptist a lot of hot air?

Does James know what he was talking about in James 1:6-7, or are there exceptions to that verse? If there are exceptions, then again by definition, those verses in James become false in themselves.

Come now, you logical and rational ones, tell me what is going on here.

If you won't tell me, then I'll tell you what is happening. I'll show you what John was doing in fashioning that answer as a question. John was BEING who he was called to BE.

Look at the second verse of Matthew chapter eleven.

> *Now when John heard in the prison the works of Christ, he sent two*
> *of his disciples, and said unto him, Art thou he that should come, or*
> *do we look for another.*
>
> *Matthew 11:2-3*

This was John's last public proclamation of the Lord. Now, let us look at the first public proclamation John made of Jesus.

> *The next day John seeth Jesus coming unto him, and saith, Behold*
> *the lamb of God, which taketh away the sin of the world.*
>
> *John 1:29*

OK, let's put these side by side, and highlight the first few words of each proclamation.

John's 1st Proclamation   John's Last Proclamation

"The next day John seeth…and saith"   **"Now when John heard…and said"**

Do we get the picture? Let me illustrate what's going on here.

John's 1st Proclamation   John's Last Proclamation
"…John seeth…"   **"…John heard…"**

"…and saith…"   "…and said…"

"For all to hear"   "For all to hear and see"

The first time John the Baptist <u>saw</u> Jesus he said <u>for all to hear.</u> The last time John <u>heard</u> and said <u>for all to see</u> (Note: The message Jesus gave back to John's disciples, "…go and shew John those things which ye do hear and see"; Matthew 11:4).

John's 1st Proclamation   John's Last Proclamation

He saw and said for all to hear.   **He heard and said for all to see.**

The cycle is complete!

From before his first breath to his very last breath John the Baptist was proclaiming this Jesus of Nazareth to be the Christ. John's life was full of one thing and one thing only, the person of Jesus Christ. John and the Lord were of the same mind (Notice: Jesus reacted immediately to what John was up to when he too asked questions about John that were answers in themselves, thus giving a hint to those, "…that hath ears to hear,…" Matthew 11:15). Therefore, in his last hours, John found one last way to proclaim Jesus as Lord. He fashioned a question that was an answer to itself, so that only those to whom it was intended would know the answer. After all:

> *… from the days of John the Baptist until now the kingdom of*
> *heaven suffereth violence, and the violent take it by force.*
> *Matthew 11:12*

Who are these to whom John directed his question? Who are these that take "heaven by force"? Volume two will deal with what is involved in taking "heaven by force". However, being one of these isn't for everyone, just as John's question wasn't for everyone. Taking "heaven by force" is only for those; to whom it may concern.

ADDENDUM I

REFERENCE CHAPTER SEVEN; p. 38

It looks as if Matthew 5:17-18 and Colossians 2:14 stand in direct opposition to one another, but these two scriptures, in fact, fully support one another.

Jesus states in Matthew 5:17-18 that he is, "…not out to destroy the law or the prophets". Yet, according to Colossians 2:14, three years later, this very same Jesus, "blotted out the handwriting of ordinances" (the law). In one he says, No, no I will never destroy the law. In the other he says I just did it.

If these two scriptures stand in opposition to one another then Jesus cannot be divine. In fact, Jesus can't even qualify to be a prophet. For, Deuteronomy states for a person to be a prophet his prophecies must be true. If any of his prophecies aren't fulfilled then the authorities are compelled to put that false prophet to death (Deuteronomy 18:20). If Colossians 2:14 is in opposition to Jesus' teachings in Matthew 5:17-18 then Jesus deserved to die at the hands of the chief priests.

However, Colossians 2:14 does in fact fulfill Matthew 5:17-18. They are not in opposition to one another. Let me illustrate by using an earthly example: The sending of a letter.

Let's say, I want to send a letter to my Father who lives in another land. I write the words that I want him to see and hear. I fold the letter; and place it in an envelope. I address the envelope. Now, I go to the post office to mail it, but the Post Master won't accept the letter for mailing. Why not?

Oh, that's easy…There is no stamp on the envelope.

Oh, how silly of me. Of course, every letter must have a stamp on it.

OK, I buy the proper postage. However, this stamp cost me everything I own, because my Father lives in a very special and wonderful place. Only the most expensive stamp ever can be used to send this envelope. Nevertheless, it is worth every penny, because I want my Father to see and hear what I have to say to him. It means everything to me.

Now, I hand the stamped envelope to the Post Master. However, he still won't mail it. Why?

Well, let me see…

Hum…let me think.

Come on now tell me why the letter won't be mailed. You know, but you are not thinking.

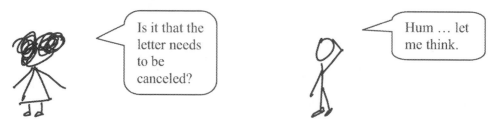

Exactly! Not only must an envelope have a stamp on it, but that stamp has to be canceled.

Cancellation means the stamp is authentic. It also means the stamp can't be used more than once. Cancellation proves the letter is official and that this letter cannot be messed with or tampered with.

Now, tell me. Did the stamp disappear when it was canceled?

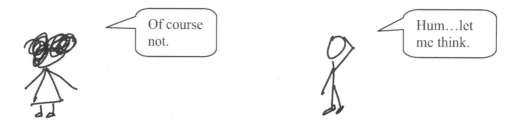

No, the stamp does not disappear. In fact, the stamp only has value when it is canceled. Up until the point of cancellation the letter is still in my possession. However, once the stamp and envelope are canceled, then, at that point, that letter becomes the possession of the U.S. Post Office. Not even the sender can tamper with the letter, because it is not mine anymore, even though I wrote the letter. This is good. Do you know why it's good the letter is no longer yours?

Once the U.S. Post Office takes control of the letter, that letter becomes absolutely secure, and at that very moment we are guaranteed delivery. We can count on it.

> *...this is the confidence that we have in him, that, if we ask*
> *any thing according to his will, he heareth us: And if we*
> *know that he hear us, whatsoever we ask, we know that we*
> *have the petitions that we desired of him.*
>
> *1 John 5:14, 15*

No matter how bad things get, we know the Post Office will get the letter delivered. It's safe in their hands. It is a sure thing.

Likewise, with God: If we have the proper stamp, in the name of Jesus, and that stamp has been canceled, covered in the blood of Jesus, then our prayers will get to God the Father. That is a guarantee. That is an absolute. However, we must truly turn over our prayers (letter) over to God's postal service. The letter (prayer) must leave our possession, and be given completely over to his possession.

Hope you noticed one thing: The stamp never disappeared, nor was it destroyed. In addition, please note the stamp gains value when it is covered in red ink. The stamp represents the law and the prophets. The law was our way back to God, but no one could pay the price for the total fulfillment of the law. No one had enough money. Only God had enough money to pay the price. Therefore, God became man with the explicit purpose of paying the price.

However, the price was only good in the form of blood (The color of ink on a canceled stamp is red: the same color as blood). Therefore, the Lamb of God had to die. Thus, our prayers get to God the Father via the life of Jesus: the stamp (Son of Man), and the death of Jesus (Son of God) the cancellation.

> *Forasmuch as ye know that ye were not redeemed with*
> *corruptible things, as silver and gold...but with the*
> *precious blood of Christ...*
> *1 Peter 1:18-19*

Two things must be present for our prayers to be heard by God: 1. We must come to God in the name of Jesus (his life, the stamp). 2. We come to God covered in the blood of Jesus (his death, the cancellation).

Yes, Matthew 5:17-18 and Colossians 2:14 indeed complement one another. We give thanks not only for the life of Jesus (fulfillment of the law and prophets); but most of all for his death (the price paid). For, it is through his death that his life has true value. Most of all, however, I thank God for the empty tomb, because one day I will no longer have to send prayers to my Father in heaven. I will be with him.

[One major caution: This illustration simplifies prayer too much. However, to clarify the two scriptures above, I had to break prayer down to its basic elements which is not desirable; for it makes prayer out to be a technique, which is wrong. Prayer is a lifestyle; a way of life; a relationship; not something to be defined and categorized as I just did. Also, the above illustration implies that prayer is outward and upward. It is not. Prayer is an inward and unceasing journey to where soul meets spirit].

REFERENCE CHAPTER TEN; p. 48

When the Roman Empire conquered a nation it was common practice for Caesar to keep in place some of the local authorities. However, for the privilege of maintaining their position, each local authority would have to pay tribute money to Caesar. In Israel's case Caiaphas, the high priest, was the Jewish local authority that was in place by Rome.

Caesar would also place in that territory one of his own special men to oversee the local authority, and to collect the tribute money from them. In this case the overseer or Governor was Pontius Pilate. Therefore, Caiaphas and Pontius Pilate were at direct odds with one another. If Caiaphas did not pay the tribute money to Pilate, Caesar would order Pilate to eliminate Caiaphas, and replace him with another high priest that would pay properly.

There was an up side to being high priest. Once the tribute money was paid to Caesar, the high priest could keep any money that was left over, and you can be sure there was always plenty of money left for Caiaphas.

Where did Caiaphas get his money? He got it from the people, of course. It is in God's law, given to Moses, three times a year all Jewish men were required to go to Jerusalem to worship in the temple. Once a year, at Passover, they were to pay their tithe. Also, Moses' law stated there can be no images brought into the temple. This presented a problem to the multitude, because the everyday money they used was Roman money which had the image of Caesar on it. Consequently, they could not pay their tithe to God in Roman money. The high priest, however, had money changers present where each man could exchange their Roman money with Caesars' image for temple money that had no image. After exchanging each man could then pay his tithe to God.

That wasn't so bad except for the fact that Caiaphas would not exchange one Roman coin for one temple coin. He had to get his tribute money for Caesar from somewhere, so Caiaphas would alter the exchange rate to coincide with how much he owed Caesar.

An example would be as follows: Suppose you figured your tithe for the past year to be one hundred dollars. You came to Jerusalem on Passover as required; went to the temple to exchange your Roman money for temple money; but found that your Roman money you worked so hard for was worth only 1/10 of temple money (as set by Caiaphas). That means to pay your one hundred dollar tithe you had to give the money changers one thousand Roman dollars. You had no choice, either pay your tithe or Caiaphas would have you thrown in jail or worse.

Another way Caiaphas made money was with the animal sacrifices the people had to make each year. Moses' law stated each male was required to give a sacrifice each year for their sins. If he failed to do so the high priest could again have him thrown into jail until he did offer proper sacrifice. Also, the sacrifice had to be without blemish.

Here is an example: During the year you save your very best lamb or dove for the Passover sacrifice. It was a perfect dove, and you were proud to be able to go to Jerusalem to sacrifice this dove for your sins. When you arrived at the temple to sacrifice the dove, the officials would inspect the dove, and say it was not a perfect dove without blemish. But you were sure it was, however they insisted. What do you do? Well, they just happened to have a perfect dove without blemish you could buy from them so you could make your sacrifice to God for your sins. For only one hundred more dollars the dove was yours. Outraged, you pay the money, knowing the price for a perfect dove was only ten dollars. They gave you their dove, and took yours. The next person behind you had the same problem. He too had to pay one hundred dollars for a dove without blemish. They took his dove and handed the man your dove you had just forfeited.

Everyone knew what these robbers were doing, but nobody could do anything about it. They had turned the temple of God into, "...a den of thieves" (Matthew 21:13).

When all was said and done, Caiaphas would take the profit; give what he must to Caesar; and pocket the rest. Consider a million or more pilgrims came to Jerusalem each Passover, and Caiaphas was a rich man. There was nothing Pontius Pilate could do to stop Caiaphas; because Caesar liked Caiaphas and his money. As long as Caiaphas paid Caesar, Pilate could only helplessly watch; and there was nothing the people could do short of a revolt. Therefore, year after year Caiaphas and his accomplices became richer and more powerful. That is, until this Jesus of Nazareth came into the picture.

That last week, Jesus came into Jerusalem sitting on a donkey. He entered the temple and cleared out the money changers.

> *And Jesus went into the temple of God, and cast out all them that*
> *sold and bought in the temple, and overthrew the tables of the*
> *money changers, and the seats of them that sold doves. And said*
> *unto them, It is written, My house shall be called the house of*
> *prayer; but ye have made it a den of thieves.*
> *Matthew 21:12-13*

He did one more thing: He stayed in the temple teaching the multitude from sunup to sundown. He would return the next day; and the next; right up to Passover day. For those four critical days Caiaphas wasn't making any money at all. By then Caiaphas was frantic.

If Caiaphas didn't make this years payment, Caesar would order a delighted Pilate to have Caiaphas' head. The people were ecstatic with this man from Galilee. Finally, someone had guts enough to stand up to Caiaphas. Jesus was a real man. Therefore, the people gladly listened to this Jesus of Nazareth. As long as Jesus remained at the temple the people didn't get ripped off.

Caiaphas tried one last way to get ride of this Jesus. He would ask Jesus a question in such a way so whichever answer Jesus would give it would be a wrong answer.

> *Then went the Pharisees, and took counsel how they might*
> *entangle him in his talk...Tell us therefore, What thinkest*
> *thou? Is it lawful to give tribute unto Caesar, or not?*
> *Matthew 22:15-17*

Now, Jesus was the one in trouble. If Jesus said, "No, we are not to pay taxes to Caesar" (Not only did the people have to pay tithes to God, each year they also had to pay taxes to Rome), then Pilate would be forced to come and drag Jesus to jail. Jesus would be gone, and Caiaphas would reinstate the money changers. If Jesus said, "yes, we are to pay our taxes to Caesar", then the people would be disappointed in Jesus. They would leave discouraged that Jesus wasn't what they thought he was. Without the multitude, Caiaphas could reinstate the money changers, and business would be back to normal again.

Everyone waited for Jesus answer. What would it be; yes or no? Either way he was doomed, or was he.

But Jesus perceived their wickedness, and said, Why tempt ye me,
ye hypocrites? Shew me the tribute money. And they brought
unto him a penny. And he saith unto them, Whose is this image
and superscription? They say unto him, Caesar's. Then saith
he unto them, Render therefore unto Caesar the things which
are Caesar's; and unto God the things that are God's.
Matthew 22:18-21

Everyone knew what he meant. Jesus had used Caiaphas' own question to turn it back on him, and to indict Caiaphas and the money changers. Jesus was saying, don't take God's money and give it to Caesar like you are doing. Yes, pay Caesar, but pay God too; and quit keeping the rest for yourself. Caiaphas had to leave:

When they had heard these words, they marveled, and left
him, and went their way.
Matthew 22:22

Caiaphas was a dead man if this Jesus were allowed to continue. As badly as Caiaphas didn't want to kill Jesus during the feast, he was ready to do so now. However, he needed an advantage. This is where Judas came in.